HMSO
S/o
555

Transport Statistics Report

Vehicle Licensing Statistics 1994

Motor vehicles currently licensed, new registrations, goods vehicle statistics.

Published July 1995

London: HMSO

Brief extracts from this publication may be reproduced provided the source is fully acknowledged. Proposals for the reproduction of larger extracts should be addressed to the Copyright Section, Her Majesty's Stationery Office, St Crispins, Duke Street, Norwich, NR3 1PD.

Governmental Statistical Service

A service of statistical information and advice is provided to the Government by specialist staffs employed in individual Departments. Statistics are made generally available through their publications and further information and advice on them can be obtained from the Departments concerned

Enquiries about the contents of this publication should be made to:

Department of Transport
STA2 Division
Room A615
Romney House
43 Marsham Street
London SW1P 3PY
Telephone: 0171 276 8559

The Department of Transport is often prepared to sell unpublished data. Further information can be obtained from the above address.

Produced from camera ready copy supplied by the Department.

The price of this publication has been set to contribute to the preparations costs incurred at the Department of Transport.

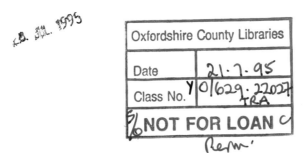

CONTENTS   PAGE

Motor vehicles registered for the first time - historic series

International comparisons of vehicle stock

Goods vehicles statistics

VEHICLE LICENSING STATISTICS 1994

Motor vehicles currently licensed, new registrations, goods vehicle statistics.

Introduction

This is the 3rd edition of "Vehicle Licensing Statistics" and is published in the same basic format as the 1993 edition, but includes some additions and improvements which readers may find helpful.

In the commentary and charts, a section has been added to provide further details on motorcars, particularly to illustrate differences between company and private ownership, and to provide extra information on diesel powered motorcars which have increased to make up about 7.5% of all motorcars by the end of 1994.

In the tables, table 4 has been expanded to show when currently licensed stock was first registered by individual years rather than two year periods. Table 7 has been similarly expanded and further subdivided to show diesel and petrol driven motorcars separately. Minor additions have been made to tables 5 and 11.

Full technical explanations of census methods, taxation and other issues are given in the notes and definitions section beginning on page 49. In the November 1994 budget, the Chancellor announced various proposals to amend and simplify the vehicle taxation system. These changes will not come into operation until 1st July 1995 and do not effect the results contained in this report.

Commentary and charts

Licensed vehicle stock 1984-1994

- The total vehicle stock in Great Britain at the end of 1994 was estimated to be 25.23 million vehicles, of which 21.20 million vehicles, or about 84%, were motorcars. The next most numerous vehicle group by <u>body type</u> was light goods vehicles with a stock of over 1.95 million vehicles, or nearly 8% of the total.

- The remainder of the stock is made up of 720,000 motorcycles; 580,000 other goods vehicles; 290,000 agricultural tractors; 150,000 buses and coaches; 30,000 three wheelers; 30,000 custom built taxis; and 280,000 other assorted vehicle types. Note that a vehicle's body type is not always a reliable guide to its taxation class.

- The final group of 280,000 other assorted vehicle types includes emergency service vehicles such as fire engines and ambulances, road repair vehicles such as road surfacers, road surface strippers, bulldozers, tar sprayers, road rollers and line painters, road maintenance vehicles such as street cleansing, snow ploughs and gritting lorries and various types of construction vehicles, cranes, shovels, diggers and excavators.

- The total stock of vehicles has grown by an estimated 22.9% between the end of 1984 and the end of 1994; a rate equivalent to 2.1% per annum. Growth has been lower in recent years. Since the end of 1989, the estimated total growth in vehicle stock is 5.4%; a rate equivalent to 1.1% per annum.

- Growth in motorcar stock totalled 30.8% between 1984 and 1994, equivalent to 2.7% per annum, and totalled 8.7% between 1989 and 1994 equivalent to 1.7% per annum..

- The stock of vehicles with goods body types remained relatively constant between 1984 and 1987, grew by about 5.5% between the end of 1988 and the end of 1989, and has since declined. The stock at the end of 1994 was 575,000 vehicles, an estimated overall reduction of 8.8% since 1984, and a reduction of 13.5% since 1988.

- Motorcycle stocks have declined steadily over the last ten years, by an estimated 46.0% in total, a rate equivalent to 6.0% fewer vehicles per year. The overall reduction of more than 600,000 motorcycles helps explain why total vehicle stocks have grown more slowly than motorcar stocks.

Licensed vehicle stock 1984-94: By body type

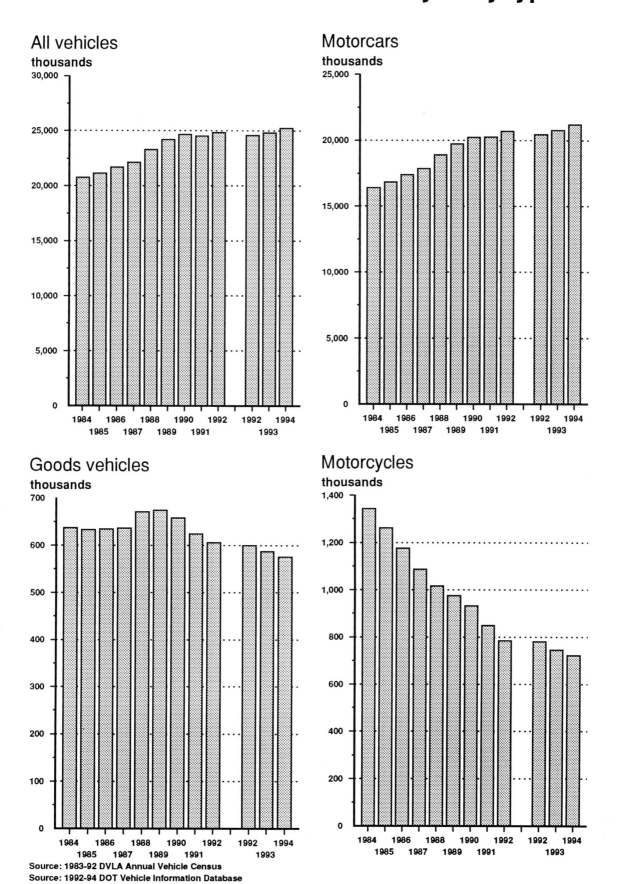

All vehicles
thousands

Motorcars
thousands

Goods vehicles
thousands

Motorcycles
thousands

Source: 1983-92 DVLA Annual Vehicle Census
Source: 1992-94 DOT Vehicle Information Database

Vehicles registered for the first time 1984 to 1994

- In a typical year somewhere between 2.0 and 2.5 million new vehicles are registered at the Driver and Vehicle Licensing Agency. In the past ten years, most vehicles were registered in 1988 and 1989 with 2.72 and 2.83 million vehicles and least in 1991 and 1992 when 1.92 and 1.90 million vehicles were registered respectively. Registrations in 1994, at 2.25 million, were 8% higher than the 1993 figure, and slightly exceeded the 1984 total of 2.24 million. Most new registrations are not additions to current stocks but replacements for existing stock.

- Registrations of new motorcars followed a similar pattern, with peaks in 1988 and 1989 and a trough in 1991 and 1992. Registrations in 1994, at 1.91 million, were 8.4% higher than in 1984. Between 1983 and 1993 the proportion of new vehicles registered to a keeper with a company title has increased from 39% to 52%, while the residue, registered to private keepers has reduced by the corresponding amount.

- New vehicles registered in goods vehicle taxation classes also reached their highest levels in 1988 and 1989 with 63 and 65 thousand new registrations respectively, and low points in 1991 and 1992 with 29 thousand new registrations in each of those two years. The relative gap between these high and low points was much greater than for other vehicle types. Registrations in 1994 at 41 thousand vehicles were 25% higher than in 1993, but remained 17% below the 1984 figure and 36% below the 1989 peak.

- Although registrations of new motorcycles showed little change between 1987 and 1988 and even increased slightly in 1989, registrations have shown a considerable overall decline in the ten year period from 1984. The number of new motorcycles registered in 1994 at 64.6 thousand was nearly 11% higher than the figure for 1983, but still 56% lower than in 1984. Whilst, in part, this may reflect consumer choice, motorcycle driving tests have also become more difficult and learner motorcyclists subject to additional regulations as the government, as part of its road safety policy, has tried to reduce the number of motorcyclists killed and injured on Britain's roads.

- In 1982 two part motorcycle tests were introduced and provisional motorcycle licenses restricted to two years. In 1983 learner motorcyclists were only allowed to ride machines up to 125 cc's. In 1989 accompanied motorcycle testing became mandatory. In 1990 compulsory basic training for learner motorcyclists was introduced, and learner motorcyclists were banned from carrying pillion passengers.

4

Vehicles registered for the 1st time 1984-94

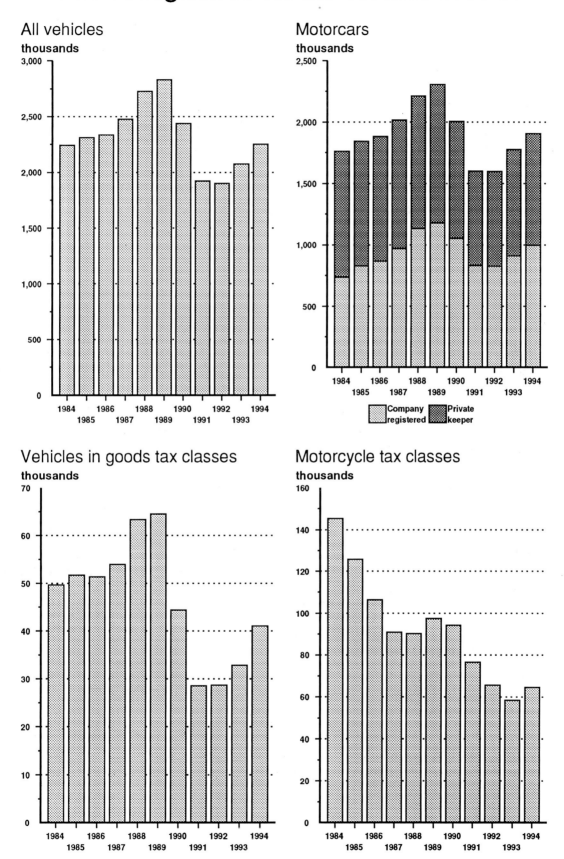

All vehicles
thousands

Motorcars
thousands

Company registered   Private keeper

Vehicles in goods tax classes
thousands

Motorcycle tax classes
thousands

5

Vehicle details: 1984 and 1994 compared

- Compared with 1984, motorcars in 1994 have a greater proportion of vehicles with engine capacities in the range 1501 to 2000 cc's, and somewhat smaller proportion with engine capacities in other groups. One explanation for this may be the increased proportion of diesel powered motorcars in use, which has risen from almost none in 1984 to 7.4% in 1994, and looks set to increase further, given that, throughout 1994, diesel vehicles made up on average 22% of new cars registered each month.

- The taxation group "hackney" for public transport vehicles, covers both taxis and buses and coaches. Compared with 1984 a smaller proportion of such vehicles fall in the group having up to four seats, that is small taxi and hackney carriages, and increased proportions into the group having from 5 to 8 seats, that is larger taxis, and the group having 9 to 32 seats, which includes minibuses and smaller buses and coaches. The proportion of larger buses and coaches, that is with 48 or more seats is little changed.

- The reduction in hackney taxation vehicles with four seats or fewer does not necessarily reflect a corresponding fall in taxi and hire car numbers. In London taxis are licensed (that is registered) via the Public Carriage Office. In provincial England and Wales taxis are licensed by district councils, who may also optionally license private hire cars. In Scotland taxis are licensed at the discretion of district and island councils, though councils which opt to license taxis must also license private hire cars. Subject to these restrictions many taxis and private hire vehicle pay vehicle excise duty in the private and light goods taxation group.

- In the period between 1984 and 1994 the bus industry has been subject to major changes, mainly as a consequence of the 1985 Transport Act, which provided for the deregulation of bus services outside London and the privitisation of the national bus company.

- The greatest change in the composition of goods vehicle stock between 1984 and 1994 has been the marked increase in the proportion of vehicles in the gross weight range from 33 to 38 tonnes, as a result of changes in regulations introduced in May 1983 which increased the maximum gross vehicle weight limit from 32.5 tonnes to 38 tonnes. This, and a slight increase in the proportion of lorries in the gross weight range up to 7.5 tonnes, is mirrored by a general fall in the proportion of general goods vehicles in other weight ranges.

- As the section on licensed stock showed, the overall stock of motorcycles has roughly halved between 1984 and 1994. Accompanying this change in numbers has been a marked upward shift in the average engine capacity of bikes in use. The proportion having engine capacities up to 50 cc's has fallen by about 17 percentage points, whereas the proportion with capacities over 500 cc's has increased from less than 10% to nearly 30% of licensed stock.

Vehicle details: 1984 and 1994 compared

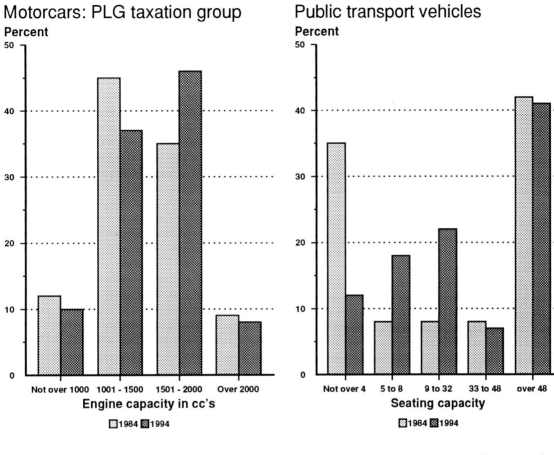

Motorcars: PLG taxation group

Percent

Engine capacity in cc's

1984 1994

Public transport vehicles

Percent

Seating capacity

1984 1994

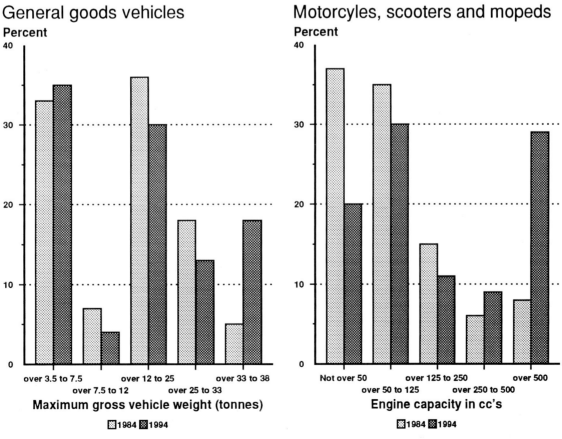

General goods vehicles

Percent

Maximum gross vehicle weight (tonnes)

1984 1994

Motorcyles, scooters and mopeds

Percent

Engine capacity in cc's

1984 1994

Current vehicle stock: Year of first registration

- Very few vehicles are not new when first registered. For all practical purposes therefore the year of first registration can be used to monitor the age of any sample of vehicles. For example, vehicles first registered in 1994 will, in general, be not more than one year old by the end of that year, vehicles first registered in 1993 not more than two years old at the end of 1994, etc etc.

- The age profile of most vehicles reflects the peak in new registration which occurred in 1989. Despite wastage, the group of motorcars more than 5 years old but not more than 6 years old remains the largest at almost 10% of licensed stock. Of currently licensed motorcars nearly 16% are not more than two years old, but about 1.5% were registered before 1978, and are now at least 17 years old.

- Among the common vehicle types, public transport vehicles have the largest group of old vehicles, with about 11% registered before 1978, and now at least 17 years old. Other age groups are roughly evenly distributed, albeit with some peaking in the 1986 to 1989 period.

- Although motorcycles are generally among the most short lived of all vehicles, older bikes were registered in substantially greater numbers than in recent years. For example, in 1980 and 1981 a combined total of over 570,000 new bikes were registered compared with a combined total of 123,000 in 1993 and 1994. Despite wastage, substantial numbers of these older bikes remain in the currently licensed stock so that even vehicles registered in 1980 still make up over 4% of current stocks.

Current vehicle stock: Year of 1st registration

Motorcars: PLG taxation group

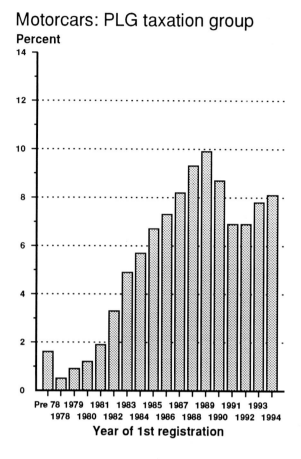

Percent

Year of 1st registration

Public transport vehicles: over 8 seats

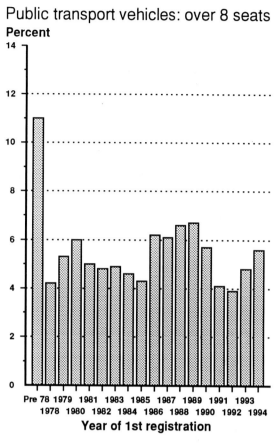

Percent

Year of 1st registration

General goods vehicles

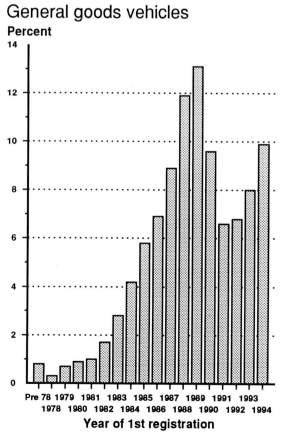

Percent

Year of 1st registration

Motorcycles, scooters and mopeds

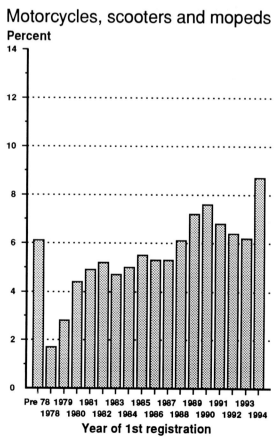

Percent

Year of 1st registration

Goods vehicle stock 1994

- Tables 18 onwards in this report give details of the currently licensed "goods vehicle stock". Although tabulations giving information on vehicles in goods vehicle taxation classes, and having goods vehicle construction are useful, they have some disadvantages.

- For example, some special vehicles may be in goods vehicle taxation groups and weigh less than 3,500 kgs, which would normally result in being taxed in the Private and Light Goods group. Moreover, some heavy goods vehicles may be taxed in other groups.

- Tables 18 onwards give statistics for a carefully defined set of currently licensed goods vehicles, all of which exceed 3,500 kgs maximum gross vehicle weight. The vehicles included are all those in taxation groups 1 to 9 (the most common heavy goods vehicle taxation groups) plus vehicles with goods vehicle body types in taxation group 26 (goods electric), taxation group 60 (crown vehicles) and taxation groups 65 to 90 (exempt vehicles).

- The goods vehicle stock, defined in this way, stood at 416,000 vehicles at the end of 1993, of which 312,000 were rigid vehicles and 103,000 articulated. This is a rise of 1.5% 1993 and is the first year to show an increase following a period of decline from the 1989 peak of 478,000 vehicles.

- Many goods vehicles are constructed to maximise the amount of goods that can be carried within regulations and taxation bands. Rigid 2 axle goods vehicles cannot exceed 17 tonnes, rigid 3 axle goods vehicles cannot exceed 24.39 tonnes and rigid 4 axle goods cannot exceed 30.49 tonnes. The maximum weight for 4 axle articulated goods vehicles is 33 tonnes, and for 5 axle articulated goods vehicles 38 tonnes. Articulated vehicles with six axles are permitted a maximum gross vehicle weight of up to 44 tonnes provided they are engaged in Combined Transport operations only. The maximum weight vehicle that can be driven on an ordinary driving license in 7.5 tonnes.

- Two axle vehicles remain the most common form of rigid lorry. Two axle articulated tractor units outnumber 3 axle units by more than two to one. Most articulated tractors are licensed to pull either 3 axle trailers, or any axle trailer configuration. Articulated vehicle trailers do not need to be registered with DVLA and are not subject to vehicle excise duty. They are, however, subject to Vehicle Inspectorate road-worthiness tests, and from this source, the total stock in 1994 is estimated at roughly 226,000 trailers.

Goods vehicle stock 1994: Weight & axle details

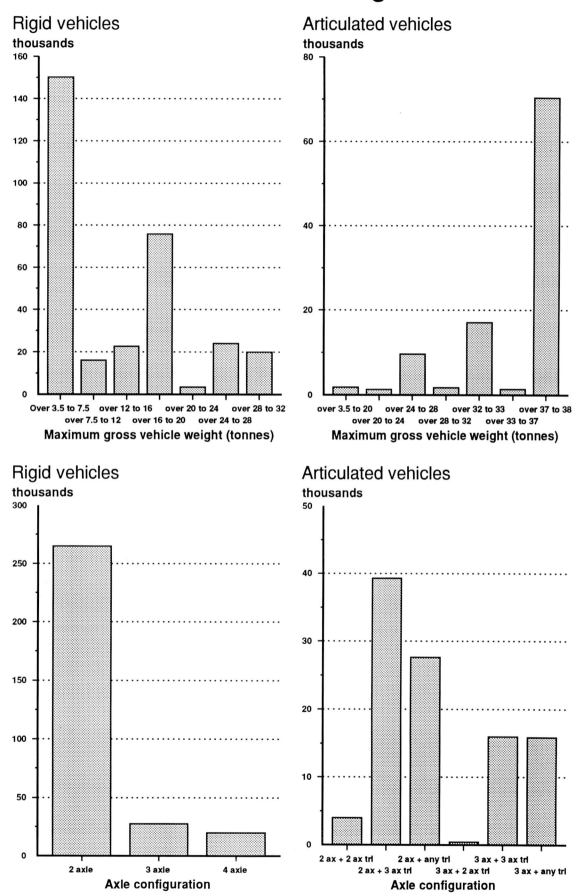

Rigid vehicles

thousands

Maximum gross vehicle weight (tonnes)

Over 3.5 to 7.5 · over 7.5 to 12 · over 12 to 16 · over 16 to 20 · over 20 to 24 · over 24 to 28 · over 28 to 32

Articulated vehicles

thousands

Maximum gross vehicle weight (tonnes)

over 3.5 to 20 · over 20 to 24 · over 24 to 28 · over 28 to 32 · over 32 to 33 · over 33 to 37 · over 37 to 38

Rigid vehicles

thousands

Axle configuration

2 axle · 3 axle · 4 axle

Articulated vehicles

thousands

Axle configuration

2 ax + 2 ax trl · 2 ax + 3 ax trl · 2 ax + any trl · 3 ax + 2 ax trl · 3 ax + 3 ax trl · 3 ax + any trl

11

Currently licensed motorcars: Vehicle details

- At the end of 1994 there were some 21.20 million vehicles with car body types licensed to use GB roads. Of these, an overwhelming majority, 20.48 million cars, were taxed within the private and light goods taxation group. Most of the rest were taxed within the group of exempt vehicles, claiming exemption in the disabled driver category.

- The title code of the registered vehicle keeper showed that 2.20 million cars, or 10.4% of the total, were registered as company owned.

- Just under 6% of vehicle registered to private keepers are diesel propelled vehicles, compared with the 22% of cars registered to companies that are diesel propelled. However, companies tend to own and use newer cars than private keepers. This difference may fall as time passes, and increasing numbers of diesel driven company cars come onto the second hand market. Modern cars are almost exclusively propelled by diesel or petrol, only 0.01% being electrically or otherwise propelled.

- The engine capacity of petrol driven motorcars is, on average, lower than that for diesel driven cars. Only a very few diesel driven cars have engines smaller than 1200 cc's, whereas almost 2 million petrol driven cars have engine capacities less than 1000 cc's.

Currently licensed motorcars: Vehicle details

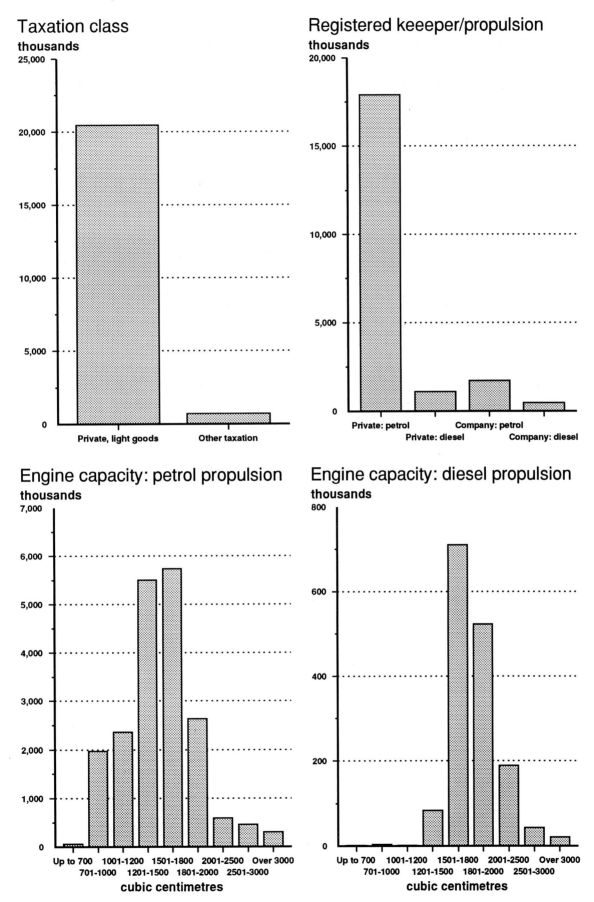

Taxation class
thousands

Private, light goods — Other taxation

Registered keeeper/propulsion
thousands

Private: petrol — Private: diesel — Company: petrol — Company: diesel

Engine capacity: petrol propulsion
thousands

Up to 700 — 701-1000 — 1001-1200 — 1201-1500 — 1501-1800 — 1801-2000 — 2001-2500 — 2501-3000 — Over 3000

cubic centimetres

Engine capacity: diesel propulsion
thousands

Up to 700 — 701-1000 — 1001-1200 — 1201-1500 — 1501-1800 — 1801-2000 — 2001-2500 — 2501-3000 — Over 3000

cubic centimetres

13

Table 1 Motor vehicles currently licensed: by taxation group: 1984-1994

Year	Private and light goods[1]		Motor cycles scooters and mopeds	Public transport vehicles[2]	Goods[3]	Special machines[4]	Other vehicles[5]	Crown and other exempt vehicles[6]	All vehicles[7]	of which body type cars	
	Body type cars	Other vehicles								All	Per cent company
1984	16,055	1,752	1,225	116	490	375	82	670	20,765	16,399	11.7
1985	16,454	1,805	1,148	120	485	374	78	695	21,159	16,829	11.8
1986	16,981	1,880	1,065	125	484	371	73	720	21,699	17,389	11.7
1987	17,421	1,952	978	129	485	374	68	744	22,152	17,856	12.2
1988	18,432	2,096	912	132	502	383	83	761	23,302	18,888	12.7
1989	19,248	2,199	875	122	505	384	77	785	24,196	19,720	13.0
1990	19,742	2,247	833	115	482	375	71	807	24,673	20,230	12.9
1991	19,737	2,215	750	109	449	346	65	840	24,511	20,253	12.0
1992[8]	20,116	2,228	688	108	437	324	59	891	24,851	20,681	11.2
1992[9]	19,870	2,198	684	107	432	324	59	903	24,577	20,444	11.1
1993	20,102	2,187	650	107	428	318	55	979	24,826	20,755	10.7
1994	20,479	2,192	630	107	434	309	50	1,030	25,231	21,199	10.4

1 For years up to 1991 retrospective counts within these new taxation classes have been estimated. See notes and definitons on taxation class changes.

2 Includes taxis.

3 Includes agricultural vans and lorries

4 Includes agricultural tractors, combine harvesters, mowing machines, digging machines, mobile cranes and works trucks.

5 Includes three wheelers, showmen's haulage and recovery vehicles.

6 Includes electric vehicles which are now exempt from licence duty.

7 The above table relates to vehicles licensed in Great Britain. The equivalant figures for Northern Ireland are given in Northern Ireland Department of Environment publication "Transport Statistics". (N.B. In 1993 586,000 vehicles were licensed in Northern Ireland of which 515,000 were in private and light goods taxation class.)

8 For the years up to 1992 estimates are taken from the annual vehicle census based on the DVLA main vehicle file.

9 From 1992 estimates of licensed stock are taken from the Department of Transport's Statistics Directorate Vehicle Information Database. See text.

Table 2 Motor vehicles currently licensed: vehicle details: 1984-94

(a) Private and light goods: [1] Body type cars within private and light goods by engine size   Thousands

Over	Not over	1984	1985	1986	1987	1988	1989	1990	1991	1992	1992	1993	1994
	700cc	128	123	120	114	108	99	90	79	71	70	62	54
700cc	1,000cc	1,832	1,891	1,963	2,022	2,145	2,205	2,215	2,163	2,109	2,084	1,998	1,905
1,000cc	1,200cc	2,109	2,128	2,153	2,154	2,201	2,215	2,226	2,198	2,232	2,207	2,227	2,261
1,200cc	1,500cc	5,043	5,076	5,115	5,111	5,259	5,361	5,418	5,358	5,411	5,349	5,330	5,337
1,500cc	1,800cc	4,030	4,278	4,573	4,850	5,279	5,641	5,872	5,944	6,105	6,025	6,129	6,276
1,800cc	2,000cc	1,524	1,556	1,616	1,718	1,920	2,162	2,352	2,465	2,655	2,622	2,841	3,088
2,000cc	2,500cc	650	665	694	710	736	747	744	726	727	719	722	759
2,500cc	3,000cc	428	433	445	448	476	501	509	498	496	489	482	486
3,000cc		308	301	301	294	307	314	315	306	309	305	312	313
cc not known[2]		3	2	1	1	1	1	1	1	-	-	-	-
All capacities		16,055	16,454	16,981	17,421	18,432	19,248	19,742	19,740	20,116	19,870	20,102	20,479
Other vehicles		1,752	1,805	1,880	1,952	2,095	2,199	2,247	2,215	2,230	2,198	2,187	2,192
All PLG		17,807	18,259	18,259	19,374	20,528	21,447	21,989	21,952	22,345	22,069	22,289	22,672

(b) Motor cycles, scooters and mopeds: by engine size   Thousands

Over	Not over	1984	1985	1986	1987	1988	1989	1990	1991	1992	1992	1993	1994
	50cc	449	423	389	352	312	280	248	207	174	173	147	129
50cc	125cc	425	402	377	347	320	303	284	249	221	222	204	187
125cc	150cc	8	6	5	4	3	3	3	2	2	2	2	2
150cc	200cc	63	54	45	39	34	31	28	24	21	22	19	18
200cc	250cc	112	99	88	78	71	68	65	60	55	55	52	50
250cc	350cc	12	12	13	13	15	16	16	15	15	15	15	15
350cc	500cc	57	53	49	46	45	45	45	42	42	41	42	45
500cc		99	98	98	99	112	131	146	150	158	155	169	186
All over 50cc		776	725	676	626	600	595	587	543	514	512	503	502
All engine sizes		1,225	1,148	1,065	978	912	875	835	750	688	684	650	630

(c) Public transport vehicles: by seating capacity   Thousands

Over	Not over	1984	1985	1986	1987	1988	1989	1990	1991	1992	1992	1993	1994
	4 seats	40.2	43.7	47.0	47.7	46.7	35.3	26.8	21.5	18.1	18.0	15.4	13.3
4 seats	8 seats	9.1	9.3	9.6	10.5	13.0	14.0	15.0	16.1	17.1	17.0	17.9	19.2
All 8 seats or less		49.3	53.0	56.6	58.2	59.7	49.3	42.0	37.6	35.3	35.0	33.4	32.5
8 seats	32 seats	8.9	9.6	12.3	15.3	17.3	18.9	20.0	20.7	21.5	21.4	22.5	23.2
32 seats	48 seats	9.4	8.6	8.0	7.7	7.3	6.7	6.3	6.1	6.4	6.4	6.8	7.8
48 seats		48.7	48.6	48.0	47.9	48.2	47.3	46.2	44.8	44.6	44.4	43.9	43.5
All over 8 seats		67.0	66.8	68.4	70.8	72.8	72.9	72.5	71.5	72.5	72.2	73.3	74.5
All capacities		116.3	119.8	125.0	129.0	132.5	122.2	114.7	109.1	107.8	107.2	106.6	107.0

(d) General goods: by gross weight[3]   Thousands

Over	Not over	1984	1985	1986	1987	1988	1989	1990	1991	1992	1992	1993	1994
3.5 tonnes	7.5 tonnes	136	138	141	145	153	157	155	148	143	143	139	139
7.5 tonnes	12 tonnes	29	26	24	22	21	20	18	17	16	16	15	15
12 tonnes	25 tonnes	147	145	143	143	147	146	140	129	124	123	120	118
25 tonnes	33 tonnes	75	69	66	64	65	62	55	49	46	45	47	51
33 tonnes	38 tonnes	20	27	34	41	51	59	61	60	63	62	65	71
38 tonnes		-	-	-	-	-	-	-	-	-	-	-	-
Gross wt unknown		7	7	7	7	7	7	2	1	1	1	-	-
All vehicles		414	412	415	422	444	451	432	403	393	389	387	394

Table 2 (continued) Motor vehicles currently licensed: vehicle details: 1984-94

(e) Farmers' goods: by gross weight[3]

Thousands

Over	Not over	1984	1985	1986	1987	1988	1989	1990	1991	1992	1992	1993	1994
	3.5 tonnes	3	3	22	21	19	18	20	20	19	19	19	20
3.5 tonnes	7.5 tonnes	8	8	8	7	7	7	7	7	7	7	6	6
7.5 tonnes	12 tonnes	3	2	2	2	2	2	1	1	1	1	1	1
12 tonnes	25 tonnes	7	7	7	6	6	5	4	5	5	5	4	4
25 tonnes	33 tonnes	2	2	1	1	1	1	1	1	1	1	1	1
33 tonnes	38 tonnes	-	-	-	-	-	-	1	1	1	1	1	1
38 tonnes		-	-	-	-	-	-	-	-	-	-	-	-
Gross wt unknown		53	51	28	25	23	20	14	12	10	10	8	7
All vehicles		76	73	68	62	58	54	48	46	43	43	41	40

(f) Agricultural tractors and machinery

Thousands

	1984	1985	1986	1987	1988	1989	1990	1991	1992	1992	1993	1994
Agricultural tractors	248	247	244	245	246	241	237	221	209	210	207	202
Combine harvesters & other agricultural machinery	41	42	42	42	43	43	44	41	40	40	40	399
Mowing machines	12	11	11	11	12	12	11	8	7	7	7	6
Digging machines	38	37	37	39	42	44	43	40	36	36	35	34
Mobile cranes	9	9	9	8	9	9	9	8	7	7	7	6
Works trucks	27	27	28	29	32	34	32	29	25	25	23	21
All vehicles	375	374	371	374	383	384	376	346	324	324	318	309

(g) Other licensed vehicles

Thousands

	1984	1985	1986	1987	1988	1989	1990	1991	1992	1992	1993	1994
Three wheelers less than 450 kgs	76	72	67	62	57	53	48	43	39	39	35	32
General haulage & showman's haulage	6	6	6	6	6	5	4	3	2	2	2	2
Others[4]	-	-	-	1	20	20	20	19	18	18	17	15
All vehicles	82	78	73	68	83	77	72	65	59	59	55	50

(g) Crown and other vehicles exempt from licence duty[5,6]

Thousands

	1984	1985	1986	1987	1988	1989	1990	1991	1992	1992	1993	1994
Crown vehicles	39	39	39	39	38	38	38	36	35	36	34	34
All other exempt	631	656	681	706	722	747	770	804	855	867	945	996
All exempt vehicles	670	695	721	744	761	785	808	840	891	903	979	1030

1 Counts of vehicles in 'Private and light goods' have been estimated up to 1991.
See notes and definitions.
2 Includes a small number of vehicles classified by horsepower.
3 Analyses by gross weight are only available from 1983. Analyses by unladen weight
are available for previous years and were last published in Transport Statitics Great Britain 1975-1985.
4 From 1987 mainly recovery vehicles.
5 Includes electric vehicles which are now exempt from licence duty.
6 From 1983 includes a large number of old vehicles exempt from tax converted to the DVLA system.

Table 3 Motor vehicles currently licensed: by body type: 1984-1994

Thousands

Year	Cars	Taxis[1]	Motor cycles	Three wheelers	Light goods	Goods	Buses and coaches	Agricultural vehicles etc[2]	Other vehicles[3]	All vehicles
1984	16,399	25	1,343	71	1,560	637	149	345	234	20,765
1985	16,829	25	1,262	62	1,606	633	148	344	248	21,157
1986	17,389	26	1,176	60	1,670	634	149	340	256	21,699
1987	17,856	28	1,086	57	1,732	636	150	340	267	22,152
1988	18,888	29	1,016	54	1,863	671	155	341	286	23,302
1989	19,720	30	976	51	1,956	674	156	334	298	24,196
1990	20,230	32	932	47	1,994	658	157	328	297	24,673
1991	20,253	32	848	43	1,961	624	154	309	287	24,511
1992[4]	20,681	32	784	40	1,976	606	155	297	280	24,851
1992[5]	20,444	32	780	40	1,951	600	154	298	280	24,577
1993	20,755	32	744	36	1,943	587	153	294	282	24,826
1994	21,199	32	721	34	1,951	575	154	285	281	25,231

1 These include mainly custom built `black cab' design vehicles.

2 Includes various types of harvesters, works trucks, mobile cranes and mowing machines.

3 Examples include ambulances, fire engines, road rollers, road construction vehicles, street cleansing etc etc.

4 For the years up to 1992 estimates are taken from the annual vehicle census based upon DVLA main vehicle file.

5 From 1992 estimates of licensed stock are taken from the Depatment of Transport's Statistics Directorate Vehicle Information Database.   See text.

Table 4 Motor vehicles currently licensed 1994: By year of first registration

(a) Private and light goods: Body type cars within private and light goods by engine size   Thousands

Over	Not over	Pre 1978	1978	1979	1980	1981	1982	1983	1984	1985
	700cc	1.6	0.4	1.2	1.2	2.0	3.5	3.5	3.7	5.0
700cc	1,000cc	43.9	14.6	24.3	34.7	77.1	91.6	130.9	146.9	160.5
1,000cc	1,200cc	50.5	16.7	31.5	43.4	57.1	95.8	125.3	154.6	164.1
1,200cc	1,500cc	86.6	25.3	43.7	77.8	117.7	202.7	293.8	328.8	364.0
1,500cc	1,800cc	58.5	17.1	28.2	44.2	71.6	173.0	283.7	342.4	446.9
1,800cc	2,000cc	23.9	7.7	16.8	21.3	27.7	54.4	89.4	100.8	131.1
2,000cc	2,500cc	17.5	7.5	13.6	15.6	21.9	32.9	45.2	48.4	51.5
2,500cc	3,000cc	17.4	4.3	8.3	8.5	10.1	19.2	27.5	27.0	30.5
3,000cc		30.4	5.1	6.4	7.2	8.2	10.1	12.6	14.1	16.7
cc not known		0.2	-	-	-	-	-	-	-	0.1
All capacities		330.5	98.7	174.2	253.9	393.5	683.4	1,011.7	1,166.8	1,370.4
Other vehicles		74.4	11.2	18.9	24.7	27.5	47.0	79.4	103.6	137.8
All PLG		404.9	109.9	193.0	278.6	421.1	730.4	1,091.1	1,270.4	1,508.2

(b) Motor cycles, scooters and mopeds: by engine size   Thousands

Over	Not over	Pre 1978	1978	1979	1980	1981	1982	1983	1984	1985
	50cc	4.1	1.0	2.3	4.2	6.4	9.5	8.7	9.9	11.4
50cc	125cc	7.4	2.1	4.1	5.8	6.2	9.7	11.7	13.0	14.1
125cc	150cc	0.7	-	0.1	0.1	-	-	-	-	-
150cc	200cc	3.5	0.8	1.5	2.4	2.5	1.1	0.7	0.6	0.5
200cc	250cc	3.9	1.7	3.4	7.0	6.8	4.5	1.6	1.0	0.8
250cc	350cc	2.2	-	-	0.3	0.6	0.3	0.4	0.5	0.6
350cc	500cc	5.9	1.8	2.0	3.1	2.8	2.9	1.9	1.3	1.5
500cc		11.1	3.5	4.1	4.9	5.5	4.9	4.9	5.5	5.7
All over 50cc		34.7	9.9	15.3	23.5	24.5	23.4	21.1	21.8	23.2
All engine sizes		38.8	10.9	17.6	27.8	30.9	32.9	29.9	31.6	34.6

(c) Public transport vehicles: by seating capacity   Thousands

Over	Not over	Pre 1978	1978	1979	1980	1981	1982	1983	1984	1985
	4 seats	0.5	0.4	0.5	0.6	0.9	1.3	1.0	1.4	1.3
4 seats	8 seats	0.3	0.1	0.1	0.2	0.3	0.3	0.3	0.3	0.3
All 8 seats or less		0.8	0.5	0.6	0.8	1.2	1.6	1.2	1.7	1.6
8 seats	32 seats	0.2	-	-	0.2	0.2	0.3	0.4	0.6	1.0
32 seats	48 seats	1.3	0.4	0.5	0.3	0.2	0.2	0.3	0.2	0.2
48 seats		6.7	2.6	3.3	3.9	3.3	3.1	3.0	2.7	2.0
All over 8 seats		8.2	3.1	4.0	4.5	3.7	3.6	3.7	3.4	3.2
All capacities		9.1	3.6	4.6	5.3	4.9	5.2	4.9	5.1	4.8

(d) General goods:by gross weight   Thousands

Over	Not over	Pre 1978	1978	1979	1980	1981	1982	1983	1984	1985
3.5 tonnes	7.5 tonnes	1.3	0.6	1.2	1.6	1.8	2.9	4.4	5.9	8.6
7.5 tonnes	12 tonnes	0.4	-	0.2	0.2	0.2	0.3	0.4	0.6	0.9
12 tonnes	25 tonnes	1.0	0.4	0.9	1.1	1.1	2.2	4.0	5.9	7.6
25 tonnes	33 tonnes	0.3	0.2	0.4	0.4	0.4	0.8	1.2	1.8	2.4
33 tonnes	38 tonnes	-	-	0.2	0.2	0.2	0.5	1.2	2.4	3.3
38 tonnes		-	-	-	-	-	-	-	-	-
Gross weight unknown		-	-	-	-	-	-	-	-	-
All vehicles		3.1	1.4	2.8	3.4	3.8	6.6	11.2	16.7	22.8

Table 4 (continued)

(a) Private and light goods: Body type cars within private and light goods by engine size   Thousands

Over	Not over	1986	1987	1988	1989	1990	1991	1992	1993	1994	All
	700cc	7.0	7.2	5.7	4.1	1.9	0.9	1.0	1.4	1.9	53.1
700cc	1,000cc	176.5	190.6	211.7	181.9	138.1	91.9	55.3	65.2	69.0	1,904.6
1,000cc	1,200cc	167.6	170.4	174.1	181.6	177.6	152.0	162.6	168.8	167.7	2,261.2
1,200cc	1,500cc	391.1	424.9	486.0	522.6	473.0	367.1	375.9	384.3	371.6	5,337.0
1,500cc	1,800cc	501.6	558.9	621.5	648.6	560.6	464.9	439.5	497.8	516.6	6,275.7
1,800cc	2,000cc	150.7	216.4	277.6	349.4	319.8	259.8	297.2	365.8	378.3	3,088.1
2,000cc	2,500cc	60.0	61.6	56.8	54.4	45.6	39.5	42.4	56.5	88.4	759.4
2,500cc	3,000cc	31.4	33.9	45.6	54.3	45.3	30.2	27.8	28.4	36.9	486.4
3,000cc		15.9	17.8	25.2	26.9	23.5	16.7	19.6	27.0	29.6	313.1
cc not known		-	-	-	-	-	-	-	-	-	0.9
All capacities		1,501.9	1,681.7	1,904.1	2,023.8	1,785.4	1,423.0	1,421.4	1,595.1	1,660.0	20,479.5
Other vehicles		164.9	193.6	230.9	245.9	204.1	150.0	152.7	149.6	176.3	2,192.5
All PLG		1,666.8	1,875.2	2,135.0	2,269.7	1,989.5	1,573.1	1,574.1	1,744.7	1,836.3	22,671.9

(b) Motor cycles, scooters and mopeds: by engine size   Thousands

Over	Not over	1986	1987	1988	1989	1990	1991	1992	1993	1994	All
	50cc	10.0	9.4	9.4	9.8	9.1	7.1	5.6	4.7	6.1	128.8
50cc	125cc	13.9	13.2	14.4	15.8	15.7	11.6	10.1	8.6	9.7	187.0
125cc	150cc	-	-	-	-	-	-	-	-	-	1.6
150cc	200cc	0.2	0.2	0.5	0.6	0.7	0.5	0.4	0.3	0.6	17.5
200cc	250cc	1.0	1.1	1.7	2.6	3.0	2.2	2.4	2.3	3.2	50.0
250cc	350cc	1.0	1.0	1.1	1.0	1.1	1.0	1.1	1.1	1.4	14.7
350cc	500cc	1.3	1.3	1.4	1.7	2.1	2.7	3.0	3.0	5.4	45.0
500cc		6.2	6.9	9.9	13.6	16.4	17.6	17.6	19.4	28.4	185.7
All over 50cc		23.6	23.8	29.0	35.4	38.9	35.6	34.5	34.7	48.7	501.6
All engine sizes		33.6	33.2	38.3	45.2	48.0	42.8	40.1	39.4	54.9	630.4

(c) Public transport vehicles: by seating capacity   Thousands

Over	Not over	1986	1987	1988	1989	1990	1991	1992	1993	1994	All
	4 seats	1.8	1.4	0.7	0.5	0.4	0.2	-	-	0.2	13.3
4 seats	8 seats	0.5	1.2	2.8	2.2	2.6	2.0	1.9	1.7	2.1	19.2
All 8 seats or less		2.3	2.7	3.4	2.8	3.0	2.2	2.0	1.8	2.2	32.5
8 seats	32 seats	2.8	3.3	2.9	2.4	2.1	1.7	1.4	1.7	2.0	23.2
32 seats	48 seats	0.1	0.1	0.2	0.2	0.4	0.3	0.7	0.8	1.2	7.8
48 seats		1.7	1.2	1.9	2.3	1.8	1.0	0.9	1.1	1.0	43.5
All over 8 seats		4.6	4.6	4.9	5.0	4.3	3.0	2.9	3.6	4.1	74.5
All capacities		6.9	7.2	8.4	7.7	7.3	5.2	5.0	5.4	6.4	107.0

(d) General goods:by gross weight   Thousands

Over	Not over	1986	1987	1988	1989	1990	1991	1992	1993	1994	All
3.5 tonnes	7.5 tonnes	9.7	12.2	15.8	17.3	14.0	9.9	9.8	10.0	12.1	139.3
7.5 tonnes	12 tonnes	1.2	1.3	1.4	1.7	1.5	1.0	1.1	1.3	1.0	14.6
12 tonnes	25 tonnes	9.0	11.5	14.9	16.0	12.0	7.4	7.1	7.4	8.0	117.5
25 tonnes	33 tonnes	3.2	4.3	6.1	6.7	4.1	3.0	3.2	4.9	7.7	51.1
33 tonnes	38 tonnes	4.0	5.9	8.7	10.0	6.3	4.6	5.6	7.8	10.2	71.1
38 tonnes		-	-	-	-	-	-	-	-	0.1	0.2
Gross weight unknown		-	-	-	-	-	-	-	-	-	0.2
All vehicles		27.1	35.2	46.8	51.7	37.9	25.9	26.9	31.5	39.1	394.0

Table 4 (continued)

(e) Farmers' goods: by gross weight

Thousands

Over	Not over	Pre 1978	1978	1979	1980	1981	1982	1983	1984	1985
	3.5 tonnes	1.2	0.4	0.5	0.8	0.9	0.7	1.1	1.4	1.9
3.5 tonnes	7.5 tonnes	0.7	0.2	0.3	0.3	0.3	0.4	0.5	0.6	0.6
7.5 tonnes	12 tonnes	0.2	-	-	-	-	-	-	-	-
12 tonnes	25 tonnes	0.3	-	0.2	0.2	0.2	0.3	0.4	0.4	0.5
25 tonnes	33 tonnes	-	-	-	-	-	-	-	-	-
33 tonnes	38 tonnes	-	-	-	-	-	-	-	-	-
38 tonnes										
Gross weight unknown		2.7	-	0.1	0.1	0.2	0.7	0.7	0.6	0.5
All vehicles		5.0	0.8	1.2	1.5	1.6	2.2	2.9	3.2	3.8

(f) Agricultural tractors and machinery

Thousands

	Pre 1978	1978	1979	1980	1981	1982	1983	1984	1985
Agricultural tractors	38.0	6.5	6.6	5.6	6.0	8.1	9.4	9.7	10.5
Combine harvesters and other agricultural	6.0	0.6	0.7	0.7	0.8	1.1	1.4	1.5	1.8
Mowing machines	-	-	-	-	-	-	0.1	0.1	0.2
Digging machines	2.4	0.5	0.7	0.6	0.5	0.8	1.0	1.1	1.2
Mobile cranes	1.6	0.2	0.3	0.3	0.2	0.2	0.2	0.2	0.2
Works trucks	1.1	0.3	0.4	0.4	0.4	0.5	0.7	0.8	0.8
All vehicles	49.1	8.2	8.8	7.6	7.9	10.7	12.8	13.4	14.7

(g) Other licensed vehicles

Thousands

	Pre 1978	1978	1979	1980	1981	1982	1983	1984	1985
Three wheelers less than 450 kgs	5.9	1.5	1.9	2.0	1.6	2.4	2.3	2.2	1.9
General haulage & showman's haulage	0.2	-	-	-	-	-	0.1	0.1	0.1
Others	2.0	0.4	0.7	0.9	0.7	1.1	1.2	1.2	1.2
All vehicles	8.1	2.0	2.7	3.0	2.4	3.5	3.6	3.6	3.3

(g) Crown and other vehicles exempt from licence duty

Thousands

	Pre 1978	1978	1979	1980	1981	1982	1983	1984	1985
Crown vehicles	5.6	0.5	0.5	0.7	0.6	0.8	0.8	0.9	1.4
All other exempt	224.8	9.1	12.3	15.4	18.6	29.3	44.6	49.7	44.4
All exempt vehicles	230.4	9.6	12.8	16.1	19.2	30.0	45.3	50.6	45.7

Table 4 (continued)

(e) Farmers' goods: by gross weight   Thousands

Over	Not over	1986	1987	1988	1989	1990	1991	1992	1993	1994	All
	3.5 tonnes	1.8	1.7	1.8	1.8	1.4	0.9	0.7	0.6	0.5	20.0
3.5 tonnes	7.5 tonnes	0.5	0.5	0.4	0.3	0.2	-	-	-	-	6.1
7.5 tonnes	12 tonnes	-	-	-	-	-	-	-	-	-	1.0
12 tonnes	25 tonnes	0.4	0.4	0.3	0.3	0.1	-	-	-	-	4.3
25 tonnes	33 tonnes	-	-	0.1	-	-	-	-	-	-	0.9
33 tonnes	38 tonnes	-	-	-	-	-	-	-	-	-	0.7
38 tonnes											
Gross weight unknown		0.4	0.4	0.3	0.3	0.2	-	-	-	-	7.2
All vehicles		3.4	3.0	3.1	2.8	2.0	1.1	0.8	0.8	0.7	40.0

(f) Agricultural tractors and machinery   Thousands

	1986	1987	1988	1989	1990	1991	1992	1993	1994	All
Agricultural tractors	8.1	8.9	11.4	11.2	10.8	9.9	9.9	13.8	17.5	202.0
Combine harvesters and other agricultural	1.7	1.8	2.2	2.5	2.4	2.3	2.7	3.6	5.1	38.9
Mowing machines	0.2	0.3	0.5	0.7	0.8	0.7	0.9	0.8	1.0	6.5
Digging machines	1.5	2.1	3.4	3.4	2.7	2.1	1.9	2.9	5.4	34.2
Mobile cranes	0.2	0.2	0.4	0.5	0.4	0.2	0.1	0.1	0.2	5.6
Works trucks	1.0	1.6	2.5	2.9	1.6	1.0	0.8	1.3	3.5	21.5
All vehicles	12.7	14.8	20.4	21.1	18.7	16.2	16.3	22.5	32.6	308.7

(g) Other licensed vehicles   Thousands

	1986	1987	1988	1989	1990	1991	1992	1993	1994	All
Three wheelers less than 450 kgs	1.9	1.7	1.7	1.2	1.0	0.1	1.0	0.7	0.6	31.9
General haulage & showman's haulage	0.2	0.2	0.2	0.2	0.2	-	-	-	-	2.2
Others	1.1	1.0	1.4	0.8	0.6	0.3	0.2	0.2	0.3	15.5
All vehicles	3.2	2.9	3.4	2.3	1.8	0.5	1.3	1.1	1.0	49.6

(g) Crown and other vehicles exempt from licence duty   Thousands

	1986	1987	1988	1989	1990	1991	1992	1993	1994	All
Crown vehicles	1.4	1.8	1.7	2.5	2.5	2.3	3.2	2.7	3.8	33.6
All other exempt	44.8	46.9	52.4	53.2	44.5	36.3	74.6	90.4	104.6	996.0
All exempt vehicles	46.3	48.7	54.0	55.7	47.0	38.6	77.8	93.1	108.4	1,029.6

Table 5 Motor vehicles currently licensed 1994: by propulsion type

Thousands

Taxation class:	Petrol	Diesel	Electric	Others[1]	All
Private and light goods	20,008.4	2,661.2	-	-	22,671.9
of which: body type cars	18,944.5	1,533.1	-	1.9	20,479.5
Motor cycles, scooters and mopeds	629.8	0.6	-	-	630.4
Farmers' goods vehicles	11.2	28.8	-	-	40.0
General goods vehicles	2.9	391.1	-	-	394.0
Public transport vehicles	5.7	101.3	-	-	107.0
Agricultural tractors and machinery	6.9	300.4	-	1.4	308.7
Other licensed vehicles	34.4	15.2	-	-	49.6
Exempt vehicles	828.0	176.6	22.7	2.3	1,029.6
All vehicles	21,527.3	3,675.1	22.7	6.1	25,231.3
of which:					
body type cars: All	19,620.9	1,576.2	-	2.0	21,199.2
body type cars: Company	1,720.1	476.5	-	0.6	2,197.3

1   Includes steam powered, gas and petrol/gas.

Table 6 Motorcars[1] currently licensed: 1988, 1991, & 1994: age distribution of stock and vehicle survival rate

Thousands/percentage

Age of vehicle		1988		1991		1994	
		Currently licensed (thousands)	Survival rate percentage	Currently licensed (thousands)	Survival rate percentage	Currently licensed (thousands)	Survival rate percentage
Over	Not over						
	2 years	4,067	96	3,433	95	3,439	93
2 years	4 years	3,505	94	4,197	93	2,946	92
4 years	6 years	3,315	93	3,543	91	3,892	90
6 years	8 years	2,713	88	3,139	87	3,670	87
8 years	10 years	2,381	74	2,652	78	2,947	79
10 years	12 years	1,414	49	1,595	53	2,248	63
12 years	14 years	596	24	888	27	1,111	36
14 years		714	. .	619	. .	0,503	. .
All ages[2]		18,886		20,252		21,199	

1   Vehicles with car body types in all taxation classes.

2   For a small number of cars the age of the vehicle is unknown.

Table 7 Motorcars currently licensed 1994: By year of first registration

Vehicles with car body types in all taxation classes: by cyclinder capacity

Petrol propulsion   Thousands

Over	Not over	Pre 1978	1978	1979	1980	1981	1982	1983	1984	1985
	700cc	3.3	0.4	1.2	1.2	2.0	3.6	3.6	3.8	5.1
700cc	1,000cc	61.3	15.0	24.9	35.5	78.8	93.7	134.2	150.4	163.5
1,000cc	1,200cc	61.8	17.2	32.3	44.3	58.5	97.8	127.9	157.7	167.1
1,200cc	1,500cc	97.5	26.0	44.9	79.8	121.3	209.1	303.4	338.9	373.8
1,500cc	1,800cc	65.6	17.7	29.4	45.8	72.3	174.9	288.2	337.6	429.5
1,800cc	2,000cc	26.9	7.9	17.4	22.1	28.6	56.4	90.9	100.1	128.5
2,000cc	2,500cc	21.7	7.6	13.8	15.7	22.0	32.6	41.9	43.0	45.1
2,500cc	3,000cc	21.5	4.5	8.7	8.8	10.5	19.6	27.7	27.3	29.9
3,000cc		36.8	5.1	6.5	7.2	8.0	9.8	12.5	14.2	16.4
cc not known		0.5	-	-	-	-	-	-	-	0.1
All capacities		397.0	101.4	179.0	260.4	402.0	697.6	1,030.6	1,173.2	1,359.1

Diesel propulsion

Over	Not over	Pre 1978	1978	1979	1980	1981	1982	1983	1984	1985
	700cc	-	-	-	-	-	-	-	-	-
700cc	1,000cc	-	-	-	-	-	-	-	0.5	0.6
1,000cc	1,200cc	-	-	-	-	-	-	-	-	-
1,200cc	1,500cc	-	0.1	0.3	0.3	-	0.1	0.1	-	0.1
1,500cc	1,800cc	-	-	-	0.2	1.9	4.5	5.8	16.3	30.6
1,800cc	2,000cc	0.2	-	0.1	0.1	0.2	0.1	1.7	4.2	6.4
2,000cc	2,500cc	1.6	0.3	0.6	0.8	1.0	1.9	5.2	7.5	8.1
2,500cc	3,000cc	0.3	-	-	0.1	0.1	0.4	0.7	0.7	1.5
3,000cc		1.1	0.2	0.3	0.3	0.6	0.7	0.7	0.6	0.6
cc not known		-	-	-	-	-	-	-	-	-
All capacities		3.4	0.8	1.4	1.9	4.0	7.8	14.4	30.0	48.2

All propulsion types (includes electricity, steam, gas and petrol/gas)

Over	Not over	Pre 1978	1978	1979	1980	1981	1982	1983	1984	1985
	700cc	3.4	0.5	1.2	1.3	2.1	3.6	3.7	3.9	5.1
700cc	1,000cc	61.3	15.0	24.9	35.5	78.8	93.7	134.3	150.9	164.1
1,000cc	1,200cc	61.8	17.2	32.3	44.4	58.5	97.9	128.0	157.8	167.2
1,200cc	1,500cc	97.6	26.1	45.2	80.1	121.4	209.2	303.5	339.0	373.9
1,500cc	1,800cc	65.7	17.7	29.4	46.0	74.2	179.4	294.0	353.9	460.2
1,800cc	2,000cc	27.1	8.0	17.5	22.2	28.8	56.5	92.6	104.3	135.0
2,000cc	2,500cc	23.3	7.9	14.4	16.5	23.0	34.4	47.2	50.5	53.2
2,500cc	3,000cc	21.8	4.5	8.8	8.9	10.6	20.1	28.5	28.0	31.4
3,000cc		37.9	5.3	6.8	7.5	8.6	10.5	13.2	14.8	17.0
cc not known		0.6	-	-	-	-	-	-	0.1	0.1
All capacities		400.5	102.3	180.4	262.3	406.0	705.4	1,045.1	1,203.3	1,407.3

Table 7 (continued)

Vehicles with car body types in all taxation classes: by cyclinder capacity

Petrol propulsion

Thousands

Over	Not over	1986	1987	1988	1989	1990	1991	1992	1993	1994	All
	700cc	7.1	7.3	5.7	4.0	1.8	0.9	1.0	1.4	1.8	55.2
700cc	1,000cc	180.0	194.2	216.1	185.7	141.0	94.4	58.5	69.7	74.7	1,971.5
1,000cc	1,200cc	170.7	173.8	177.8	185.6	181.2	156.3	182.4	185.8	183.0	2,361.3
1,200cc	1,500cc	401.3	435.1	497.6	532.5	480.3	372.7	395.3	397.9	394.1	5,501.9
1,500cc	1,800cc	474.8	529.3	592.4	610.0	519.5	413.5	367.9	393.2	378.3	5,739.9
1,800cc	2,000cc	146.4	203.2	261.3	323.2	289.1	224.7	236.0	242.5	227.0	2,632.3
2,000cc	2,500cc	53.1	51.1	43.3	41.6	33.1	25.4	24.9	30.0	49.4	595.2
2,500cc	3,000cc	30.4	33.2	43.3	51.4	41.6	25.9	24.1	23.4	25.6	457.4
3,000cc		15.5	17.6	24.8	26.3	23.0	16.3	17.1	22.5	25.4	305.0
cc not known		-	-	-	-	-	-	-	-	-	1.2
All capacities		1,479.4	1,644.9	1,862.3	1,960.4	1,710.6	1,330.0	1,307.2	1,366.3	1,359.4	19,620.9

Diesel propulsion

Thousands

Over	Not over	1986	1987	1988	1989	1990	1991	1992	1993	1994	All
	700cc	-	-	-	-	-	-	-	0.1	0.2	1.1
700cc	1,000cc	0.4	0.4	0.4	0.2	0.2	0.2	0.3	0.2	0.1	3.7
1,000cc	1,200cc	-	-	0.1	0.2	0.1	0.2	0.2	0.2	0.3	1.8
1,200cc	1,500cc	0.1	0.1	0.3	3.0	4.7	3.9	7.4	30.6	32.3	83.6
1,500cc	1,800cc	40.0	43.3	43.7	53.1	53.0	60.6	85.9	117.7	153.2	709.8
1,800cc	2,000cc	8.5	18.6	22.9	33.3	36.5	39.2	65.8	128.2	156.3	522.3
2,000cc	2,500cc	8.6	12.0	14.8	13.8	13.1	14.6	18.0	27.0	40.2	189.1
2,500cc	3,000cc	1.8	1.5	3.2	3.7	4.3	4.6	3.9	5.2	11.4	43.6
3,000cc		0.6	0.5	0.7	1.0	0.7	0.7	2.7	4.8	4.2	21.0
cc not known		-	-	-	-	-	-	-	-	-	0.2
All capacities		60.0	76.4	86.0	108.4	112.7	124.0	184.5	314.1	398.2	1,576.2

All propulsion types (includes electricity, steam, gas and petrol/gas)

Thousands

Over	Not over	1986	1987	1988	1989	1990	1991	1992	1993	1994	All
	700cc	7.1	7.3	5.7	4.1	1.9	0.9	1.1	1.5	2.0	56.3
700cc	1,000cc	180.3	194.6	216.5	185.9	141.2	94.6	58.8	69.9	74.8	1,975.2
1,000cc	1,200cc	170.8	173.8	177.9	185.7	181.4	156.5	182.6	186.1	183.4	2,363.3
1,200cc	1,500cc	401.5	435.2	497.8	535.6	485.0	376.6	402.8	428.5	426.4	5,585.7
1,500cc	1,800cc	514.8	572.6	636.1	663.2	572.4	474.1	453.8	510.9	531.7	6,450.1
1,800cc	2,000cc	154.8	221.8	284.2	356.6	325.5	263.9	301.9	370.7	383.5	3,154.8
2,000cc	2,500cc	61.7	63.2	58.1	55.4	46.2	40.0	42.8	57.0	89.6	784.4
2,500cc	3,000cc	32.2	34.6	46.4	55.1	45.9	30.5	28.0	28.6	37.3	501.3
3,000cc		16.2	18.0	25.5	27.3	23.8	17.0	19.9	27.3	30.2	326.7
cc not known		-	-	-	-	-	-	-	-	-	1.5
All capacities		1,539.5	1,721.3	1,948.3	2,068.9	1,823.4	1,454.1	1,491.7	1,680.5	1,759.0	21,199.2

Table 8 Motor vehicles currently licensed: by taxation group: region: 1994

Thousands

	Private and light goods		Motor cycles scooters and mopeds	Public transport vehicles[1]	Goods[2]	Special machines[3]	Other vehicles[4]	Crown and other exempt vehicles[5]	All vehicles	of which: body type cars	
County region country	Body type cars	Other vehicles								All	Per cent company
Cleveland	169.0	16.3	4.2	0.5	3.2	2.2	0.5	12.8	208.7	179.3	4.3
Cumbria	178.8	20.5	6.4	0.8	5.2	8.1	0.6	11.9	232.1	185.6	8.6
Durham	170.3	17.6	3.8	1.3	4.0	3.3	0.5	16.3	216.9	183.9	4.6
Northumberland	90.0	8.8	2.2	0.2	1.8	3.8	0.2	5.3	112.4	93.8	4.2
Tyne and Wear	281.5	27.7	4.4	2.3	5.3	1.8	0.6	21.3	345.0	299.5	8.5
Northern	889.6	90.9	20.9	5.1	19.5	19.3	2.3	67.6	1115.2	942.1	6.5
Humberside	270.2	27.9	15.6	1.1	6.6	7.5	1.1	13.4	343.4	279.6	6.7
North Yorkshire	261.2	32.2	11.5	0.8	8.9	14.3	0.8	13.7	343.4	267.4	7.3
South Yorkshire	407.1	44.5	10.9	2.7	9.9	4.5	1.5	31.9	513.0	434.0	7.0
West Yorkshire	648.2	73.8	14.2	2.7	18.7	4.7	2.1	38.1	802.5	675.4	11.6
Yorks & H'side	1586.6	178.4	52.2	7.3	44.1	31.0	5.5	97.2	2002.3	1656.3	8.9
Derbyshire	277.9	35.2	9.7	1.8	7.1	4.7	1.1	14.7	352.1	287.4	11.5
Leicestershire	321.0	34.2	10.5	1.3	6.5	4.4	1.0	13.2	392.1	329.5	11.0
Lincolnshire	227.5	26.6	9.8	1.0	6.4	15.0	0.9	14.1	301.2	235.4	6.6
Northamptonshire	219.2	22.2	7.2	1.0	7.0	3.0	0.5	9.8	269.8	224.7	11.6
Nottinghamshire	357.0	38.4	12.6	1.2	8.2	4.8	1.1	21.6	444.8	373.8	7.8
East Midlands	1402.5	156.7	49.8	6.2	35.2	31.9	4.5	73.3	1760.0	1450.8	9.7
Cambridgeshire	284.8	33.5	11.5	1.0	7.0	8.5	0.7	12.2	359.3	291.4	11.5
Norfolk	308.1	36.3	15.4	1.2	6.4	11.9	1.0	14.7	395.0	316.0	8.8
Suffolk	259.6	28.5	13.4	0.7	7.5	7.6	0.9	12.7	330.8	267.0	6.1
East Anglia	852.5	98.4	40.3	2.9	20.9	27.9	2.6	39.6	1085.1	874.3	8.9
Bedfordshire	212.1	21.8	5.8	1.0	3.8	2.6	0.4	7.7	255.3	216.5	11.2
Berkshire	389.1	36.2	9.6	1.0	5.4	2.4	0.6	9.3	453.7	394.5	20.2
Buckinghamshire	282.3	23.1	6.9	0.4	6.4	2.7	0.4	8.3	330.5	287.1	16.7
East Sussex	256.8	26.5	8.2	1.3	2.9	2.0	0.7	9.3	307.6	263.2	4.8
Essex	611.2	65.5	19.8	2.9	10.3	6.8	1.4	23.5	741.5	626.7	5.9
Greater London	2297.6	221.2	63.9	21.8	34.9	4.6	3.2	69.3	2716.3	2342.9	16.0
Hampshire	646.7	63.4	25.2	1.5	8.1	6.0	1.4	25.4	777.6	660.2	8.0
Hertfordshire	492.2	47.8	13.9	2.0	8.9	3.8	0.8	13.3	582.7	500.1	12.9
Isle of Wight	46.6	5.6	2.6	0.2	0.5	0.6	0.2	2.2	58.6	48.0	2.6
Kent	592.1	60.5	22.4	2.7	9.7	6.9	1.8	24.1	720.2	606.5	6.4
Oxfordshire	230.0	23.5	9.9	0.8	4.1	4.0	0.5	7.4	280.2	233.8	7.6
Surrey	450.1	43.1	13.2	1.5	7.0	2.3	0.7	12.9	530.7	456.4	8.1
West Sussex	308.0	30.2	9.1	0.4	2.9	2.8	0.6	9.1	363.0	313.8	9.0
South East	6814.8	668.4	210.5	37.5	104.8	47.5	12.6	221.7	8117.8	6949.7	11.8
Avon	372.1	40.3	15.8	1.5	8.0	2.9	1.0	13.3	454.9	380.4	8.4
Cornwall	178.6	23.5	9.1	1.0	3.2	6.3	0.8	11.3	233.7	185.3	3.7
Devonshire	390.0	48.8	19.0	2.1	6.8	11.0	1.3	18.3	497.2	401.5	4.9
Dorset	278.9	29.6	11.8	1.1	3.2	4.4	0.7	10.7	340.3	285.7	4.5
Gloucestershire	228.6	24.4	10.0	0.7	3.8	3.9	0.6	9.7	281.8	234.1	6.7
Somerset	189.3	23.0	8.3	0.7	7.3	6.5	0.6	8.9	244.7	194.0	5.1
Wiltshire	294.0	28.9	10.8	0.6	6.4	4.9	0.6	10.1	356.4	299.1	24.3
South West	1931.6	218.4	84.8	7.8	38.6	40.0	5.6	82.4	2409.1	1980.1	8.6

Table 8 Motor vehicles currently licensed: by taxation group: region: 1994

Thousands

County region country	Private and light goods		Motor cycles scooters and mopeds	Public transport vehicles[1]	Goods[2]	Special machines[3]	Other vehicles[4]	Crown and other exempt vehicles[5]	All vehicles	of which: body type cars	
	Body type cars	Other vehicles								All	Per cent company
Hereford & Worcs	286.8	32.6	10.2	1.0	6.7	6.9	0.8	12.7	357.6	294.1	12.8
Salop	166.9	20.5	5.3	0.5	5.4	6.9	0.4	10.7	216.6	172.7	8.2
Staffordshire	359.4	37.4	12.6	1.8	9.0	5.4	1.2	20.9	447.8	375.6	7.4
Warwickshire	208.3	21.1	6.7	0.7	4:3	5.1	0.5	8.8	255.5	213.5	20.9
West Midlands	1024.5	143.3	20.3	4.1	27.9	4.0	2.7	47.3	1273.9	1060.3	19.1
West Midlands	2045.9	254.9	55.1	8.1	53.3	28.2	5.6	100.3	2551.5	2116.1	15.5
Cheshire	362.5	37.0	11.9	1.2	8.7	5.2	0.8	20.3	447.6	378.5	6.6
Gtr Manchester	851.3	90.4	15.6	3.8	23.3	3.5	2.1	45.1	1035.0	888.4	18.8
Lancashire	520.2	53.9	15.4	3.7	13.2	6.4	1.5	33.1	647.4	546.5	6.2
Merseyside	371.3	33.8	8.4	4.4	6.6	1.3	0.8	41.1	467.7	408.0	6.2
North Western	2105.4	215.1	51.3	13.1	51.8	16.4	5.2	139.6	2597.7	2221.4	11.3
England	17628.7	1881.1	565.0	87.9	368.1	242.2	43.8	821.7	21638.6	18190.9	11.0
Clwyd	145.2	15.9	4.4	0.5	3.5	3.2	0.4	11.5	184.5	154.3	4.4
Dyfed	123.8	17.7	3.2	0.8	4.7	5.9	0.3	12.4	168.9	131.8	3.2
Gwent	148.1	15.8	4.0	1.0	3.4	1.8	0.4	13.5	187.9	159.8	4.6
Gwynedd	83.2	11.6	2.2	0.8	2.5	3.0	0.2	6.1	109.5	87.5	3.1
Mid Glamorgan	141.3	14.4	2.9	0.9	2.8	0.9	0.3	18.1	181.6	158.1	3.9
Powys	42.4	7.9	1.1	0.2	2.6	3.9	0.1	3.3	61.5	43.9	5.1
South Glamorgan	117.0	11.0	1.7	0.5	2.1	0.5	0.2	6.1	139.2	121.7	20.7
West Glamorgan	114.9	10.9	2.7	1.0	1.6	0.7	0.3	11.6	143.7	125.1	5.3
Wales	915.9	105.3	22.1	5.6	23.2	19.9	2.2	82.5	1176.8	982.2	6.2
Borders	37.9	5.0	0.6	0.2	1.0	2.4	0.1	1.8	49.0	38.9	7.5
Central Scotland	93.8	9.2	1.3	0.4	2.8	1.4	0.2	5.6	114.7	98.4	17.1
Dumfries & Galloway	51.0	6.4	1.4	0.1	2.1	4.3	0.1	3.0	68.4	52.9	5.7
Fife	107.8	9.3	2.1	0.6	1.7	2.3	0.2	6.9	131.0	113.6	4.3
Grampian	189.8	20.3	4.5	1.2	5.2	9.0	0.3	7.1	237.4	193.7	7.8
Highland	67.7	10.2	1.8	0.4	1.8	3.2	0.2	3.9	89.1	69.9	5.2
Lothian	238.2	23.8	3.8	2.5	3.9	2.9	0.3	16.3	291.8	247.8	13.5
Orkney	7.1	1.3	0.2	0.1	0.3	1.2	0.0	0.5	10.8	7.3	4.7
Shetland	8.0	1.9	0.2	0.1	0.3	0.5	0.0	0.4	11.5	8.1	5.9
Strathclyde	586.1	54.6	6.3	5.7	13.0	7.8	0.8	49.6	724.0	629.5	8.0
Tayside	129.8	13.0	2.3	0.6	3.1	5.5	0.2	6.5	161.1	134.2	7.0
Western Isles	8.2	1.7	0.1	0.1	0.3	0.4	0.0	0.4	11.3	8.5	3.7
Scotland	1525.5	156.6	24.8	12.1	35.5	40.9	2.5	102.1	1900.0	1602.8	8.8
County unknown	42.0	3.7	1.2	0.1	0.6	0.5	0.1	1.9	50.1	43.6	6.3
No current keeper vehicle under disposal	367.3	45.7	17.3	1.2	6.7	5.2	1.0	21.4	465.8	379.6	0.0
Great Britain	20479.5	2192.5	630.4	107.0	434.0	308.7	49.6	1029.6	25231.3	21199.2	10.4

1 Includes taxis

2 Includes agricultural vans and lorries but excludes electrical goods vehicles.

3 Agricultural tractors, combine harvesters, mowing machines, digging machines, mobile cranes and works trucks.

4 Includes three wheeelers, showmen's haulage and recovery vehicles.

5 Includes electric vehicles.

Table 9 Motor vehicles currently licensed:[1] 1903-1983

For detail of years 1984-1994 see table 1

Thousands

Year	Private and light goods[2]		Goods vehicles[3,4]	Motorcycles scooters and mopeds[5]	Public transport vehicles[6]	Special machines etc[7]	Other vehicles[8]	Crown and exempt vehicles[9]	All vehicles
	Private cars	Other vehicles							
1903	8		4	..	5	..	..	..	17
1909	53		30	36	24	..	..	..	143
1920	187		101	228	75	..	..	..	591
1930	1056		349	712	101	15	15	24	2272
1939	2034		488	418	90	31	3	84	3148
1946	1770		560	449	105	146	16	61	3107
1950	1979	439	439	643	123	262	24	61	3970
1951	2095	457	451	725	123	250	26	63	4190
1952	2221	477	450	812	119	270	29	86	4464
1953	2446	516	446	889	105	289	30	88	4809
1954	2733	566	450	977	97	307	32	88	5250
1955	3109	633	462	1076	92	326	35	89	5822
1956	3437	685	471	1137	89	336	37	95	6287
1957	3707	723	473	1261	87	355	41	96	6743
1958	4047	772	461	1300	86	367	46	96	7175
1959	4416	824	473	1479	83	383	55	96	7809
1960	4900	894	493	1583	84	392	65	101	8512
1961	5296	944	508	1577	82	400	76	106	8989
1962	5776	1002	512	1567	84	401	83	107	9532
1963	6462	1092	535	1546	86	412	88	115	10336
1964	7190	1184	551	1534	86	421	90	120	11176
1965	7732	1240	584	1420	86	417	91	127	11697
1966	8210	1283	577	1239	85	399	87	142	12022
1967	8882	1358	593	1190	85	416	89	147	12760
1968	9285	1388	580	1082	89	409	92	157	13082
1969	9672	1408	547	993	92	398	90	162	13362
1970	9971	1421	545	923	93	385	89	121	13548
1971	10443	1452	542	899	96	380	92	126	14030
1972	11006	1498	525	866	95	371	95	128	14584
1973	11738	1559	540	887	96	373	97	137	15427
1974	11917	1547	539	918	96	380	96	149	15642
1975	12526	1592	553	1077	105	384	108	166	16511
1976	13184	1626	563	1175	110	387	117	156	17318
1977	13220	1591	559	1190	110	393	115	167	17345
1978	13626	1597	549	1194	110	394	111	177	17758
1979	14162	1623	561	1292	111	402	106	359	18616
1980	14660	1641	507	1372	110	397	100	412	19199
1981	14867	1623	489	1371	110	365	95	427	19347
1982	15264	1624	477	1370	111	371	91	454	19762
1983	15543	1692	488	1290	113	376	86	621	20209

1 The annual vehicle census of licensed vehicles has been taken as follows: 1903-1910 at 31 December; 1911-1920 at 31 March; 1921-1925 for the highest quarter; 1926-1938 for the September quarter; 1939-1945 at 31 August; 1946-1976 for the September quarter; 1977 census results are estimates; 1978 onward at 31 December.

2 From 1950 onwards, retrospective counts within the October 1982 taxation classes have been estimated. For years up to 1990, retrospective counts within these new taxation classes have been estimated. See Notes on taxation class changes.

3 Includes agricultural vans and lorries, showmens' goods vehicles licensed to draw trailers (note 2 applies).

4 Excludes electric goods vehicles which are now exempt from licence duty.

5 Includes scooters and mopeds.

6 Includes taxis. Prior to 1969, tram cars were included.

7 Includes agricultural tractors, combine harvesters, mowing machines, digging machines, mobile cranes and works trucks.

8 Includes three-wheelers, showmens' haulage and recovery vehicles.

9 Includes electric vehicles which are now exempt from licence duty and personal and direct export vehicles.

Table 10 Motor vehicles registered for the first time: by taxation group: 1984-94

Thousands

	Private and light goods[1]		Motor cycles scooters and mopeds	Public transport vehicles[2]	Goods[3,4]	Special machines[5]	Other vehicles[6]	All vehicles	of which body type cars[7]		
Year	Body type cars	Other vehicles							All	Per cent company	Per cent imports
1984	1,721.6	211.0	145.2	7.2	49.6	40.1	64.2	2,238.9	1,759.3	42	57
1985	1,804.0	225.5	125.8	6.8	51.7	40.1	55.4	2,309.3	1,842.1	45	57
1986	1,839.3	231.4	106.4	8.9	51.4	34.8	61.5	2,333.7	1,883.2	46	54
1987	1,962.7	249.9	90.8	8.7	54.0	37.7	70.1	2,473.9	2,016.2	48	50
1988	2,154.7	282.3	90.1	9.2	63.4	45.2	78.6	2,723.5	2,210.3	51	55
1989	2,241.2	294.0	97.3	8.0	64.5	42.5	81.4	2,828.9	2,304.4	51	55
1990	1,942.3	237.6	94.4	7.4	44.4	34.2	78.4	2,438.7	2,005.1	52	56
1991	1,536.6	171.9	76.5	5.2	28.6	26.1	76.6	1,921.5	1,600.1	52	55
1992	1,528.0	166.4	65.6	5.1	28.7	24.1	83.9	1,901.8	1,599.1	52	55
1993	1,694.6	158.8	58.4	5.4	32.8	30.0	94.0	2,074.0	1,776.5	52	55
1994	1,809.1	182.6	64.6	6.7	41.1	35.3	109.7	2,249.0	1,906.4	52	57

1 For years up to 1990 retrospective counts within these new taxation classes
  have been estimated. See notes and definitons on taxation class changes.

2 Includes taxis.

3 Includes agricultural vans and lorries and showman's goods vehicles
  licensed to draw trailers.

4 From 1981, excludes electric goods vehicles which are now exempt from licence duty.

5 Includes agricultural tractors, digging machines, mobile cranes, works trucks and mowing machines,
  but excludes all exemptions.

6 Includes Crown and exempt vehicles, three wheelers, pedestrian controlled
  vehicles, general haulage and showmen's tractors. From 1981 also includes
  electric goods vehicles which are now exempt from licence duty.

7 Cars in all taxation classes.

Table 11 Motor vehicles registered for the first time: by taxation group, vehicle details: 1984-1994

(a) Private and light goods: by engine size   Thousands

Over	Not over	1984	1985	1986	1987	1988	1989	1990	1991	1992	1993	1994
	1,000cc	227.9	225.5	236.3	245.5	260.5	222.0	162.0	104.3	64.7	73.4	78.6
1,000cc	1,200cc	223.9	217.3	205.9	198.2	195.8	196.2	183.0	153.4	176.3	180.8	184.1
1,200cc	1,500cc	526.2	507.6	508.1	520.7	576.6	600.5	531.0	406.2	412.3	415.5	415.2
1,500cc	1,800cc	578.7	669.0	689.8	723.4	782.5	799.6	681.0	557.2	521.7	576.2	623.7
1,800cc	2,000cc	189.5	220.4	234.1	312.7	387.5	462.2	403.0	321.6	344.4	405.3	427.2
2,000cc	2,500cc	94.4	95.4	104.7	111.8	108.5	109.7	102.0	104.4	115.1	135.1	184.6
2,500cc	3,000cc	43.7	44.4	43.3	45.8	57.4	66.5	56.0	38.2	34.5	33.8	43.6
3,000cc		28.5	26.9	24.6	26.2	34.6	37.2	32.7	23.2	25.3	33.3	34.5
cc not known		0.4	0.4	0.3	0.1	0.1	0.1	0.1	0.1	0.1	0.1	0.1
All vehicles		1,913.2	2,006.9	2,047.2	2,184.3	2,403.6	2,494.0	2151.7	1,708.5	1,694.2	1,853.4	1,991.6

Of which: Private and light goods: Diesel propulsion   Thousands

Over	Not over	1984	1985	1986	1987	1988	1989	1990	1991	1992	1993	1994
	1,000cc											0.6
1,000cc	1,200cc											0.4
1,200cc	1,500cc											29.4
1,500cc	1,800cc											210.9
1,800cc	2,000cc											174.9
2,000cc	2,500cc											130.0
2,500cc	3,000cc											15.7
3,000cc												6.0
cc not known												-
All vehicles												568.0

(b) Motor cycles, scooters and mopeds: by engine size   Thousands

Over	Not over	1984	1985	1986	1987	1988	1989	1990	1991	1992	1993	1994
	50cc	55.4	48.3	37.5	29.7	24.7	22.9	18.8	13.1	9.1	6.5	6.9
50cc	150cc	59.9	50.0	41.8	34.0	31.9	32.4	29.1	18.8	14.7	11.2	10.5
150cc	200cc	2.6	1.7	1.1	0.9	1.5	1.7	1.5	1.1	0.7	0.6	0.7
200cc	250cc	4.1	3.4	3.3	3.6	4.1	5.6	6.0	4.6	4.2	3.6	3.6
250cc	350cc	2.9	2.6	3.3	2.7	2.8	2.7	2.5	2.2	2.0	1.9	1.7
350cc	500cc	4.0	4.4	3.8	3.3	3.2	3.5	4.2	5.2	5.3	4.9	6.8
500cc		16.4	15.4	15.7	16.6	21.8	28.6	32.2	31.5	29.5	29.9	34.3
All vehicles		145.2	125.8	106.4	90.8	90.1	97.3	94.4	76.5	65.6	58.4	64.6

(c) Public transport vehicles: by seating capacity   Thousands

Over	Not over	1984	1985	1986	1987	1988	1989	1990	1991	1992	1993	1994
	4 seats	2.8	2.7	2.9	2.2	1.2	0.6	0.2	0.1	0.1	0.1	0.5
4 seats	8 seats	0.5	0.4	0.5	1.4	3.0	2.4	2.7	2.1	2.0	1.7	2.1
8 seats or less		3.3	3.1	3.4	3.6	4.2	3.0	2.9	2.2	2.0	1.8	2.5
8 seats	32 seats	0.7	1.3	3.5	3.6	2.7	2.4	2.5	1.6	1.6	1.7	1.9
32 seats	48 seats	0.2	0.3	0.2	0.2	0.2	0.3	0.5	0.3	0.4	0.8	1.2
48 seats		2.9	2.1	1.8	1.3	2.0	2.5	1.8	1.1	1.0	1.2	1.0
All over 8 seats		3.9	3.7	5.5	5.1	5.0	5.2	4.8	3.0	3.1	3.6	4.2
All capacities		7.2	6.8	8.9	8.7	9.2	8.2	7.7	5.2	5.1	5.4	6.7

Table 11 (Continued) Motor vehicles registered for the first time: by taxation group, vehicle details: 1984-1994

(d) Goods: by gross weight

Thousands

Over	Not over		1988	1989	1990	1991	1992	1993	1994
	3.5 tonnes		1.2	1.0	0.7	0.6	0.5	0.5	0.5
3.5 tonnes	7.5 tonnes		21.5	21.6	17.0	10.8	10.4	10.4	12.6
7.5 tonnes	12 tonnes		1.9	2.0	1.6	1.1	1.2	1.3	1.0
12 tonnes	25 tonnes		18.6	18.8	13.1	8.0	7.6	8.7	10.5
25 tonnes	33 tonnes		8.9	8.9	4.8	3.1	3.2	3.9	5.9
33 tonnes	38 tonnes		11.3	12.2	7.2	5.0	5.9	8.1	10.5
38 tonnes	40 tonnes		0.0	0.0	0.0	0.0	0.0	0.0	0.0
40 tonnes									0.1
Gross weight unknown			-	-	-	-	-	-	-
All vehicles			63.4	64.5	44.4	28.6	28.7	32.8	41.1

(e) Special machines, agricultural tractors etc.

Thousands

	1984	1985	1986	1987	1988	1989	1990	1991	1992	1993	1994
Agricultural tractors	24.5	24.3	18.6	19.6	21.8	19.3	17.6	14.6	13.9	17.7	18.3
Combine harvesters and other agricultural machinery	3.3	3.7	2.6	2.7	3.0	3.0	2.8	2.4	2.5	2.5	2.5
Mowing machines	1.8	1.5	1.8	1.8	1.8	2.0	1.7	1.1	1.2	1.0	1.1
Digging machines	4.6	4.6	5.1	6.1	8.5	7.5	5.5	3.7	2.9	3.9	5.8
Mobile cranes	0.4	0.5	0.5	0.4	0.9	0.9	0.8	0.3	0.2	0.2	0.3
Works trucks	3.3	3.5	4.0	4.9	7.0	7.4	3.7	2.3	1.7	2.1	4.1
Others	2.2	2.1	2.2	2.2	2.3	2.4	2.2	1.7	1.8	2.6	3.2
All vehicles	40.1	40.1	34.8	37.7	45.2	42.6	34.2	26.1	24.1	30.0	35.3

(f) Other licenced vehicles

Thousands

	1984	1985	1986	1987	1988	1989	1990	1991	1992	1993	1994
Three wheelers and pedestrian controlled vehicles	2.9	2.6	2.6	2.2	2.1	1.5	1.2	0.3	1.2	1.0	0.9
General haulage and showman's haulage	0.4	0.4	0.4	0.4	0.4	0.2	0.1	0.1	0.1	0.1	..
Recovery vehicles[1,2]	.	.	.	.	0.9	0.9	0.7	0.4	0.3	0.3	0.3
All vehicles	3.3	3.0	3.0	2.6	3.4	2.6	2.1	0.7	1.6	1.4	1.3

(g) Crown and other vehicles exempt from licence duty

Thousands

	1984	1985	1986	1987	1988	1989	1990	1991	1992	1993	1994
Crown vehicles	5.1	5.8	5.3	4.6	4.1	4.4	4.0	3.2	3.7	3.1	4.1
Personal and direct export vehicles	8.2	9.2	9.3	10.8	9.9	9.9	9.1	8.9	7.1	7.5	9.3
Other exempt vehicles	47.6	37.5	44.0	52.2	56.1	64.4	63.1	63.8	71.6	81.9	95.0
All exempt vehicles	60.8	52.5	58.5	67.5	70.1	78.6	76.2	75.8	82.3	92.4	108.4

1 New tax class introduced in January 1988.

2 New tax class introduced in Jan 1988. Most registrations in 1988 were vehicles previously operated on trade plates. The figure shown for that year is an estimate of new registrations.

Table 12 Motor vehicles registered for the first time: by county: 1994 with related stock and ownership information.

County region country	1984 All vehicles currently licensed (thousands)	1994 All vehicles		1994 Car in all taxation classes			
		New registrations (thousands)	Currently licensed (thousands)	New registrations (thousands)	Currently licensed (thousands)	Per 1,000 population[1]	Average vehicle age (years)[2]
Cleveland	181	16.1	208.7	12.9	179.3	320	6.7
Cumbria	190	17.5	232.1	14.0	185.6	379	6.9
Durham	174	17.1	216.9	14.3	183.9	303	6.5
Northumberland	91	9.5	112.4	8.0	93.8	305	6.3
Tyne and Wear	287	35.3	345.0	30.4	299.5	263	6.3
Northern	923	95.5	1115.2	79.5	942.1	304	6.5
Humberside	303	24.9	343.4	19.6	279.6	316	6.8
North Yorkshire	288	28.5	343.4	21.4	267.4	370	6.5
South Yorkshire	402	38.1	513.0	30.4	434.0	332	6.9
West Yorkshire	654	73.5	802.5	59.6	675.4	321	6.2
Yorks & H'side	1,647	164.9	2002.3	131.1	1656.3	330	6.5
Derbyshire	282	44.6	352.1	36.9	287.4	302	6.9
Leicestershire	334	50.6	392.1	45.1	329.5	362	7.1
Lincolnshire	260	19.1	301.2	14.5	235.4	391	7.2
Northamptonshire	216	21.5	269.8	17.5	224.7	380	6.9
Nottinghamshire	375	30.0	444.8	24.4	373.8	363	7.1
East Midlands	1,467	165.8	1760.0	138.3	1450.8	355	7.0
Cambridgeshire	280	30.7	359.3	24.6	291.4	427	7.0
Norfolk	339	27.0	395.0	21.6	316.0	413	7.4
Suffolk	281	21.6	330.8	16.6	267.0	413	7.6
East Anglia	900	79.4	1085.1	62.7	874.3	418	7.4
Bedfordshire	230	22.6	255.3	18.4	216.5	401	7.0
Berkshire	351	60.1	453.7	54.2	394.5	517	6.4
Buckinghamshire	244	47.9	330.5	42.3	287.1	441	6.4
East Sussex	277	16.7	307.6	14.3	263.2	364	7.9
Essex	634	57.7	741.5	49.2	626.7	402	7.6
Greater London	2,547	307.4	2716.3	274.5	2342.9	338	7.3
Hampshire	658	59.3	777.6	51.1	660.2	414	7.5
Hertfordshire	502	71.0	582.7	63.1	500.1	500	6.8
Isle of Wight	52	2.6	58.6	2.2	48.0	384	8.8
Kent	622	46.0	720.2	38.2	606.5	394	7.5
Oxfordshire	244	19.5	280.2	15.9	233.8	399	7.3
Surrey	486	50.9	530.7	43.2	456.4	440	7.2
West Sussex	304	26.7	363.0	22.6	313.8	437	7.4
South East	7,151	788.4	8117.8	689.1	6949.7	391	7.3
Avon	413	11.6	454.9	9.9	380.4	391	7.7
Cornwall	201	11.3	233.7	9.0	185.3	389	8.3
Devonshire	424	27.1	497.2	20.7	401.5	383	8.1
Dorset	295	17.2	340.3	13.8	285.7	428	8.2
Gloucestershire	244	16.3	281.8	13.3	234.1	430	7.7
Somerset	211	12.0	244.7	8.8	194.0	409	8.2
Wiltshire	259	49.0	356.4	44.0	299.1	513	6.4
South West	2,047	144.4	2409.1	119.5	1980.1	415	7.8

1 Using mid year 1993 population estimates.

2 Nominal: Vehicles registered at any time in 1994 are counted as age 1 at the end of 1994, vehicles registered in 1983 are counted as age 2 at the end of 1994, etc, etc.

Table 12 (continued) Motor vehicles registered for the first time: by county: 1994 with related stock and ownership information.

County region country	1984 All vehicles currently licensed (thousands)	1994 All vehicles		1994 Car in all taxation classes			
		New registrations (thousands)	Currently licensed (thousands)	New registrations (thousands)	Currently licensed (thousands)	Per 1,000 population[1]	Average vehicle age (years)[2]
Hereford & Worcs	280	31.9	357.6	27.1	294.1	423	7.2
Salop	169	14.9	216.6	11.7	172.7	417	7.2
Staffordshire	370	32.1	447.8	25.6	375.6	356	7.1
Warwickshire	178	30.0	255.5	25.2	213.5	432	6.4
West Midlands	985	177.9	1273.9	154.4	1060.3	403	6.5
West Midlands	1,982	286.8	2551.5	244.0	2116.1	400	6.7
Cheshire	366	39.1	447.6	32.1	378.5	389	6.8
Gtr Manchester	807	123.4	1035.0	107.1	888.4	345	6.2
Lancashire	543	45.2	647.4	38.0	546.5	385	6.9
Merseyside	398	37.9	467.7	32.7	408.0	283	6.9
North Western	2,114	245.6	2597.7	210.0	2221.4	346	6.6
England	18,231	1970.7	21638.6	1674.1	18190.9	375	7.1
Clwyd	151	10.4	184.5	8.6	154.3	371	7.5
Dyfed	140	10.2	168.9	8.0	131.8	375	7.5
Gwent	159	11.4	187.9	9.5	159.8	355	7.1
Gwynedd	95	5.6	109.5	4.6	87.5	364	7.6
Mid Glamorgan	146	12.2	181.6	10.5	158.1	291	6.9
Powys	52	3.5	61.5	2.4	43.9	366	7.3
South Glamorgan	139	15.4	139.2	13.7	121.7	295	6.1
West Glamorgan	121	10.8	143.7	9.2	125.1	337	7.1
Wales	1,003	79.5	1176.8	66.6	982.2	338	7.1
Borders	40	3.9	49.0	3.1	38.9	369	6.4
Central Scotland	84	11.4	114.7	9.9	98.4	361	5.8
Dumfries Galloway	58	5.4	68.4	4.1	52.9	358	6.4
Fife	105	8.9	131.0	7.6	113.6	323	6.8
Grampian	189	20.2	237.4	16.6	193.7	367	6.2
Highland	70	6.8	89.1	5.5	69.9	338	6.5
Lothian	222	28.2	291.8	23.4	247.8	329	6.1
Orkney	9	0.4	10.8	0.3	7.3	369	7.7
Shetland	9	1.0	11.5	0.7	8.1	356	6.2
Strathclyde	564	71.2	724.0	61.5	629.5	275	5.9
Tayside	130	12.6	161.1	10.4	134.2	340	6.6
Western Isles	9	0.4	11.3	0.3	8.5	288	6.7
Scotland	1,489	170.4	1900.0	143.3	1602.8	313	6.1
County unknown	3	28.4	50.1	22.3	43.6	n/a	6.8
No current keeper vehicle under disposal	-	n/a	465.8	n/a	379.6	n/a	8.3
Great Britain	20,726	2249.0	25231.3	1906.4	21199.2	375	7.0

1 Using mid year 1993 population estimates.

2 Nominal: Vehicles registered at any time in 1994 are counted as age 1 at the end of 1994, vehicles registered in 1983 are counted as age 2 at the end of 1994, etc, etc.

Table 13 Monthly vehicle registrations: Seasonally adjusted series: 1990-1994[1]

Thousands

| Year | Month | Cars | of which: | | Motor cycles | Goods | All vehicles |
			Imported cars	Company cars			
1990	January	184.4	105.8	93.5	8.4	4.5	232.2
	February	171.8	101.5	94.6	8.2	4.3	213.1
	March	175.1	102.6	93.2	8.6	3.9	220.3
	April	169.6	98.1	89.1	8.3	4.3	203.4
	May	181.7	98.9	91.1	8.6	3.8	220.7
	June	168.0	94.3	89.9	7.4	3.7	202.7
	July	165.0	91.6	89.0	7.6	3.7	203.7
	August	168.5	89.2	87.0	7.9	3.6	200.3
	September	166.8	88.7	85.4	7.3	3.6	197.5
	October	158.9	88.4	84.6	7.7	2.8	187.7
	November	151.1	82.9	80.9	7.4	3.0	181.4
	December	143.9	75.6	71.5	7.1	2.9	175.4
	All 1990	2005.1	1117.5	1049.9	94.4	44.0	2438.4
1991	January	146.3	78.5	74.5	7.6	2.8	184.3
	February	130.6	72.6	71.8	6.4	2.4	156.8
	March	149.4	80.3	76.2	7.3	2.5	181.1
	April	127.1	70.9	70.2	7.3	2.2	152.4
	May	126.2	71.2	68.3	6.8	2.4	153.7
	June	119.7	71.0	68.1	5.8	2.3	144.7
	July	129.6	74.6	73.0	6.1	2.2	160.9
	August	147.3	74.5	66.0	6.2	2.3	174.3
	September	139.9	73.7	70.1	5.8	2.4	162.9
	October	126.5	71.2	64.2	5.3	2.5	147.2
	November	129.3	69.2	66.3	6.0	2.3	151.5
	December	128.3	66.5	64.3	5.9	2.4	151.6
	All 1991	1600.1	874.2	833.1	76.5	28.6	1921.5
1992	January	129.4	68.5	69.5	6.1	2.3	154.7
	February	122.1	68.0	64.6	5.6	2.3	147.7
	March	123.9	68.9	63.4	5.4	2.5	149.1
	April	144.2	78.0	71.2	5.6	2.2	168.5
	May	130.0	72.9	68.2	5.8	2.1	156.6
	June	130.5	73.7	66.9	5.7	2.4	157.2
	July	128.0	70.9	66.4	5.8	2.7	151.7
	August	131.2	70.6	69.0	5.2	2.4	156.8
	September	130.6	70.8	66.9	4.6	2.3	153.8
	October	134.3	73.4	71.5	4.5	2.7	157.1
	November	133.3	72.5	69.3	4.5	2.5	157.4
	December	161.6	86.4	79.7	6.6	2.4	191.1
	All 1992	1599.1	874.5	826.7	65.6	28.7	1901.8
1993	January	136.2	76.1	67.6	5.4	2.2	161.9
	February	141.7	76.9	73.4	6.0	2.5	166.6
	March	140.0	76.8	74.1	5.6	2.1	164.2
	April	143.9	78.3	75.6	5.4	2.4	168.0
	May	146.6	81.0	77.6	5.4	2.5	172.0
	June	143.6	78.9	74.2	4.9	2.7	167.9
	July	147.0	83.3	72.6	4.7	2.5	168.6
	August	154.3	86.8	79.0	4.5	2.9	179.5
	September	150.6	86.5	77.6	4.0	4.2	176.4
	October	158.4	87.7	79.0	3.7	2.5	182.7
	November	161.7	91.6	81.3	4.3	3.2	188.1
	December	152.4	87.6	78.9	4.5	3.0	178.2
	All 1993	1776.5	991.5	910.1	58.4	32.8	2074.1
1994	January	167.1	91.8	84.6	6.3	2.5	194.9
	February	161.7	92.7	82.8	6.5	2.9	189.2
	March	160.4	91.8	83.2	6.0	3.2	190.0
	April	153.4	88.2	79.7	5.5	2.8	180.2
	May	160.7	89.0	81.1	5.3	3.3	189.7
	June	165.7	93.7	85.4	4.9	3.3	194.5
	July	152.6	88.7	80.7	5.1	3.4	178.3
	August	158.4	90.0	84.5	5.0	3.6	187.4
	September	159.9	90.4	87.1	4.2	3.8	188.8
	October	154.4	88.4	82.0	4.2	4.0	181.8
	November	158.6	89.4	85.6	5.6	4.5	190.1
	December	153.5	87.0	79.5	6.0	3.9	184.0
	All 1994	1906.4	1082.1	996.4	64.6	41.1	2249.0

1. Seasonal adjustment constrained to equal actual annual totals.

Table 14 Motor Vehicles registered for the first time: 1951-1983

For detail on years 1984-1994 see table 10

Thousands

Year	Private and light goods[1]	Goods vehicles[1]	Motor cycles scooters and mopeds[2]	Public transport vehicles[3]	Special machines etc[4]	Other vehicles[5,6]	All vehicles
1951	136.2	84.5	133.4	7.8	34.4	17.6	413.9
1952	187.6	81.8	132.5	5.4	35.3	16.0	458.6
1953	295.1	97.2	138.6	5.0	33.5	14.1	583.5
1954	386.4	109.6	164.6	5.5	35.2	17.1	718.4
1955	500.9	153.5	185.2	5.6	39.2	22.1	906.5
1956	399.7	148.0	142.8	5.1	31.9	23.3	750.8
1957	425.4	140.5	206.1	5.0	39.8	19.9	836.7
1958	555.3	172.6	182.7	4.9	47.2	18.9	981.6
1959	645.6	191.7	331.8	5.1	49.0	29.7	1252.9
1960	805.0	225.9	256.7	6.4	42.5	32.9	1369.4
1961	742.8	220.2	212.4	6.1	46.4	31.4	1259.3
1962	784.7	192.3	140.2	5.5	42.8	26.7	1192.2
1963	1008.6	206.4	165.5	6.4	47.9	31.2	1466.0
1964	1190.6	229.3	205.1	6.5	46.1	33.6	1711.2
1965	1122.5	229.4	150.9	6.8	45.4	45.7	1600.7
1966	1065.4	227.2	109.4	6.8	48.4	36.4	1493.6
1967	1116.7	221.5	137.7	6.5	53.9	38.9	1575.2
1968	1116.9	231.7	112.0	7.1	57.0	37.2	1561.9
1969	987.4	239.6	85.4	7.1	49.3	33.0	1401.8
1969	1133.2	93.8	85.4	7.1	49.3	33.0	1401.8
1970	1248.1	85.2	104.9	7.7	48.8	30.2	1524.9
1971	1462.1	74.2	127.9	9.5	37.9	30.0	1741.6
1972	1854.8	74.9	152.5	9.8	47.6	44.1	2183.7
1973	1851.3	82.7	193.6	10.0	49.7	43.0	2230.3
1974	1399.6	68.0	189.8	7.8	45.6	39.6	1750.4
1975	1317.2	67.0	264.8	7.8	48.5	44.6	1749.9
1976	1401.8	63.9	270.6	8.7	51.8	41.2	1838.0
1977	1445.0	68.8	251.3	8.8	48.3	39.8	1862.0
1978	1519.9	79.8	225.3	9.1	50.0	41.4	1925.5
1979	1891.5	91.3	285.9	9.1	47.7	44.4	2369.9
1980	1679.2	74.7	312.7	8.8	36.7	43.5	2155.6
1980	1699.2	54.9	312.7	8.8	36.7	43.5	2155.8
1981	1643.6	39.9	271.9	7.5	32.6	34.8	2030.3
1982	1745.5	41.2	231.6	7.1	41.2	39.6	2103.9
1983	1989.1	46.6	174.5	7.3	42.1	47.9	2307.5

1 From 1969 onwards registrations for the new October 1982 taxation
   classes have been estimated. See Notes. Figures for 1951- 1969 refer to
   previous classes. From 1980 onwards figures relate to the October 1990 taxation classes
2 Includes scooters and mopeds.
3 Includes taxis but excludes tram cars.
4 Includes trench diggers, mobile cranes, etc but excludes agricultural
   tractors on exempt licences.
5 Includes crown and exempt vehicles, three wheelers, pedestrian
   controlled vehicles, and showmens' goods vehicles.
6 Excludes vehicles officially registered by the armed forces.

Table 15 International comparisons: Vehicle stock: 1982 and 1992

Thousands

	Cars and taxis		Goods vehicles[1]		Motor cycles etc[2]		Buses and coaches		All vehicles	
	1982	1992	1982	1992	1982	1992	1982	1992	1982	1992
Great Britain	15,888[3]	21,403[3]	1,662	2,221	1,502	823[4]	72.8[5]	78.7[5]	19,125	24,526
Northern Ireland	394[3]	502[3]	38	48	16	10	2.1[5]	2.2[5]	450	562
United Kingdom	16,282[3]	21,904[3]	1,700	2,269	1,518	833	74.9[5]	80.9[5]	19,575	25,087
Belgium	3,231	4,021	227	364	510	438[6]	16.6	15.3	3,985	4,838[7]
Denmark	1,358	1,596	231	297	208	135[6]	7.8	11.3	1,805	2,039[7]
France	20,300	24,020	2,739	3,677	5,250	3,060	61.0	69.0	28,350	30,826
Former FRG	24,105	32,007	1,291	1,549	2,887	2,702	71.3	69.9	28,354	36,328
Former GDR	2,922	5,206[6]	228	274[6]	1,302	1,330[6]	53.0	63.0[6]	4,505	6,873[6]
Germany	27,027	37,213[7]	1,519	1,823[7]	4,189	4,032[7]	124.3	132.9[7]	32,859	43,201[6]
Greece	999	1,829	508	790	146	340	18.5	22.7	1,672	2,982
Irish Republic	714	864	68	145	26	25	3.0	4.6	811	1,039
Italy	19,616	28,200	1,461	2,443[6]	4,523	7,570[6]	66.7	78.0[6]	25,667	38,291[6]
Luxembourg	138	201	9	14	2	5	0.7	0.8	150	221
Netherlands	4,650	5,658	317	565	765	672	11.4	12.3	5,743	6,907
Portugal	1,420	3,050	250	590	98	160	10.0	12.8	1,778	3,813
Spain	8,354	13,102	1,462	2,650	1,283	1,252	43.0	47.2	11,142	17,051
Austria	2,361	3,245	193	269	621	516	9.2	9.4	3,184	4,039
Croatia	..	674	..	29	..	189	..	4.1	..	896
Former										
Czechoslovakia	2,283	3,476	255	241	663[8]	540[8]	32.4	40.9	3,233[8]	4,298[8]
Finland	1,352	1,936	159	263	215	64[8]	9.1	8.7	1,735	2,272[8]
Hungary	1,182	2,058	119	229	630	163[8]	25.0	22.9	1,956	2,473[8]
Norway	1,338	1,619	78	311	164	165	14.2	26.8	1,594	2,122
Sweden	2,936	3,587	190	305	17	48	13.3	14.3	3,156	3,954
Switzerland	2,473	3,099	178	276	834	732	12.0	13.5	3,497	4,121
Japan	25,539	38,964	15,441	22,619[6]	14,558	16,818	231.0	248.6	55,769	78,650[7]
USA	122,763	146,015[6]	35,523	44,785[6,9]	5,743	4,177[6]	559.0	631.3[6]	164,588	195,608[6]

Note: These data conform to UN/ECE definitions of road vehicles and do not always correspond
to the data shown in other parts of this report.

For further details and historic series see `International
Comparisons of Transport Statistics 1970-1991 Part 3:
Road vehicles, traffic, fuel and expenditure'
published by HMSO, price £16.20.

Contact point for
further information:
0171-276 8515

1 Rigid vehicles only.

2 Including mopeds and three-wheeled vehicles.

3 Including car-derived vans.

4 1991 estimate revised to 891,000.

5 Vehicles taxed as hackneys with 9 or more seats.

6 1991 data.

7 Estimated.

8 Excluding mopeds.

9 1991 estimate revised from 45,619 to 44,785 thousand.

Table 16 International comparisons: Vehicles per head: 1982 and 1992

Vehicles per 1000 head of population

	Cars and taxis		Goods vehicles[1]		Motor cycles etc[2]		Buses and coaches		All vehicles	
	1982	1992	1982	1992	1982	1992	1982	1992	1982	1992
Great Britain	290 [3]	379 [3]	30.3	39.4	27.4	14.6	1.33 [4]	1.40 [4]	349	435
Northern Ireland	263 [3]	314 [3]	25.3	30.0	10.7	6.3	1.41 [4]	1.38 [4]	300	351
United Kingdom	289 [3]	378 [3]	30.2	39.1	27.0	14.4	1.33 [4]	1.39 [4]	348	433
Belgium	326	402	22.9	36.4	51.5	44.4 [5]	1.68	1.53	402	484 [6]
Denmark	266	307	45.3	57.1	40.8	26.2 [5]	1.53	2.17	354	392 [6]
France	375	418	50.5	64.1	96.9	53.3	1.13	1.20	523	537
Former FRG	391	494	20.9	23.9	46.8	41.7	1.16	1.08	460	561
Former GDR	175	315 [5]	13.7	16.6 [5]	78.0	80.5 [5]	3.17	3.81 [5]	270	416 [5]
Germany	345	457 [6]	19.4	22.4 [6]	53.4	49.5 [6]	1.59	1.63 [6]	419	531 [5]
Greece	102	178	51.8	76.7	14.9	33.0	1.89	2.20	171	289
Irish Republic	204	240	19.4	40.3	7.4	6.9	0.85	1.27	232	288
Italy	342	496	25.5	42.3 [5]	78.9	131.0 [5]	1.16	1.35 [5]	448	663 [5]
Luxembourg	345	503	22.5	35.0	5.0	12.5	1.75	1.95	374	552
Netherlands	325	372	22.2	37.2	53.5	44.2	0.80	0.81	402	454
Portugal	143	308	25.3	59.6	9.9	16.2	1.01	1.30	180	385
Spain	221	335	38.7	67.8	33.9	32.0	1.14	1.21	295	436
Austria	315	411	25.7	34.1	82.8	65.3	1.22	1.19	425	511
Former Czechoslovakia	149	221	16.7	..	43.3 [7]	34.4 [7]	2.12	2.60	211 [7]	274 [7]
Finland	282	387	33.1	52.6	44.8	12.8 [7]	1.89	1.73	361	454 [7]
Hungary	110	200	11.1	22.2	58.9	15.8 [7]	2.34	2.22	183	240 [7]
Norway	326	377	19.0	72.3	40.0	38.4	3.46	6.22	389	493
Sweden	354	412	22.9	35.1	2.0	5.5	1.60	1.64	380	455
Switzerland	386	449	27.8	40.0	130.3	106.1	1.88	1.96	546	597
Japan	217	313	131.0	182.5 [5]	123.5	135.3	1.96	2.00	473	633 [6]
USA	530	578 [5]	153.4	177.2 [5]	24.8	16.5 [5]	2.41	2.50 [5]	711	774 [5]

Note: These data conform to UN/ECE definitions of road vehicles and do not always correspond
to the data shown in other parts of this report.

1 Rigid vehicles only.
2 Including mopeds and three-wheeled vehicles.
3 Including car-derived vans.
4 Vehicles taxed as hackneys with 9 or more seats.
5 1991 data.
7 Estimated.
8 Excluding mopeds.

Table 17 International comparisons: Road goods vehicles: 1982 and 1992

Thousands

	Rigid goods vehicles		Road tractors		Trailers and semi-trailers	
	1982	1992	1982	1992	1982	1992
Great Britain	1662	2221	90	99	205.43 [10]	236.22 [10]
Northern Ireland	38	48	2	2	5 [10]	5 [10]
United Kingdom	1,700	2,296	92	101	210	241
Belgium	227	364	18 [5]	39	59	103
Denmark[1]	231	297	11	17	157	347
France [2]	2,739	3,677	132	190 [4]	146	174 [4]
Germany	1,291	1,823	477 [4]	515 [4]	325 [4]	485 [4]
Greece	508	790	0	..	7	..
Irish Republic[3]	68	145 [6]	63	74	..	..
Italy	1,461	2,443	37	..	330	..
Luxembourg	9	14	3 [7]	8 [7]	..	16 [11]
Netherlands	317	565	24	41	77	..
Portugal	250	590	..	15	..	26
Spain	1,462	2,650	28	77	55	128
Austria	193	269	345 [4,8]	396 [4,8]	188 [4]	330 [4]
Former Czechoslovakia	255	241	..	225	..	260
Finland	159	263	3	..	27 [12]	377
Hungary	119	229	26 [9]	37 [9]	106 [9]	235 [9]
Norway	78	311	2	211	..	380
Sweden	190	305	4	6 [10]	289	449
Switzerland	178	276	2	6	63	111
Yugoslavia	211	..	301	..	..	..
Japan	15,441	22,619	38	98 [4]	60	94 [4]
USA	35253	44785	1193	1353	2676	3608

1 Including imported second-hand vehicles.

2 Vehicles less than 10 years old.

3 Vehicles with a current licence only.

4 For tractors and trailers, as published in UNECE "Annual Bulletin of Transport Statistics"
   but number of trailer figure apprears small in relation to number of tractors.

5 Vehicles which have undergone a technical inspection.

6 Number of trailers are included under rigid goods vehicles.

7 Includes special vehicles.

8 Tractors with a road registration number making more than 10 km/h and circulating on public roads(ie may include agricltural tractors.

9 Tractors and trailers with a road registration number (including agricultural vehicles.)

10 Estimated.

11 Trailers only.

12 Excluding trailers with a permissible maximum weight of 750 kg or less.

Table 18 Goods vehicle stock at end of year: 1983 - 1994

Thousands

Year	Rigid vehicles	Articulated vehicles				All vehicles
		Not over 28 tonnes	28-37 tonnes	over 37 tonnes	All	
1983	348	11	68	10	89	436
1984	347	12	60	19	91	437
1985	341	12	52	26	90	432
1986 [1]	341	13	46	34	93	435
1987	346	14	43	41	98	444
1988	357	14	40	51	105	462
1989	368	14	36	60	110	478
1990 [1]	353	14	30	63	106	460
1991	330	13	26	61	100	430
1992	316	13	23	63	99	415
1993	313	12	21	64	98	410
1994	312	13	20	71	103	416

1 The analysis was delayed until the end of January the following year. Figures therefore include vehicles newly registered (about 3,000 in 1987 and 2,000 in 1991) or scrapped during the following January.

Trailers - analysis by axle type[1]

Thousands

National totals	1 axle	2 axle	3 axle	4 axle	5 axle	Total
First / Annual tests in 1992	13.1	132.2	75.6	0.1	-	221.0
First / Annual tests in 1993	12.0	128.5	83.7	0.1	-	224.3
First / Annual tests in 1994	11.1	122.3	92.1	0.1	-	225.6

1 This table is derived from Vehicle Inspectorate data on the number of trailers tested.
  Total stock at the end of 1991 was estimated to be between 230 and 240 thousand trailers.

Table 19 Goods vehicle stock: by gross weight and axle configuration: 1994

Thousands

Tractor	Trailer	Over Not over	3.5t 7.5t	7.5t 12t	12t 16t	16t 20t	20t 24t	24t 28t	28t 32t	32t 33t	33t 37t	37t 38t	38t	All weights
Rigid vehicles														
2 Axle			150.1	15.9	22.6	75.3	0.1	0.2	0.1	0.2	0.2	-	0.2	264.9
3 Axle			0.1	-	-	0.4	3.3	23.6	-	-	0.0	-	-	27.5
4 Axle			-	-	-	-	-	0.2	19.7	-	0.0	0.0	0.0	20.0
All rigid			150.2	15.9	22.7	75.7	3.4	24.0	19.9	0.2	0.2	-	0.2	312.4
Articulated vehicles														
2 Axle	2 Axle		0.0	0.0	-	0.1	0.4	3.4	-	-	-	-	0.0	4.0
	3 Axle		0.0	0.0	-	-	-	0.3	0.1	0.6	1.0	37.2	0.0	39.4
	Any		0.2	-	0.1	1.4	0.8	5.7	1.5	16.0	0.1	1.9	0.0	27.7
All 2 Axle			0.2	-	0.1	1.5	1.2	9.4	1.7	16.6	1.1	39.2	0.0	71.0
3 Axle	2 Axle		-	0.0	0.0	-	-	-	-	0.2	0.1	-	0.0	0.4
	3 Axle		0.0	-	0.0	-	-	-	-	0.1	0.1	15.7	0.1	16.0
	Any		-	-	0.0	-	-	0.1	-	0.1	-	15.5	0.1	15.9
All 3 Axle			-	-	0.0	-	-	0.1	-	0.4	0.2	31.2	0.2	32.3
2 & 3 Axle	2 Axle		-	0.0	-	0.1	0.4	3.5	-	0.3	0.1	-	0.0	4.4
	3 Axle		0.0	-	-	-	-	0.3	0.1	0.7	1.1	52.9	0.1	55.3
	Any		0.2	-	0.1	1.4	0.8	5.8	1.6	16.1	0.1	17.4	0.1	43.5
All articulated			0.2	-	0.1	1.5	1.2	9.6	1.7	17.0	1.3	70.4	0.2	103.3

Table 20 Goods vehicle stock: by taxation group and axle configuration: 1994

Thousands

| Taxation class(es) | Rigid vehicles | | | | Articulated vehicles | | | | | | | | | | |
| | 2 axle | 3 axle | 4 axle | All | 2 axle tractor | | | | 3 axle tractor | | | | All | All |
					2 axle trailer	3 axle trailer	any trailer	All	2 axle trailer	3 axle trailer	any trailer	All		
General goods														
1 HGV	236.4	24.9	19.2	280.5	3.9	38.9	26.5	69.3	0.4	15.9	15.6	31.9	101.2	381.7
2 Trailer HGV	5.0	1.2	-	6.2	0.0	0.0	-	-	0.0	0.0	0.0	0.0	-	6.2
Farmers goods														
3 HGV	10.4	0.6	0.3	11.2	0.1	0.4	0.6	1.0	-	0.1	0.1	0.2	1.3	12.5
4 Trailer HGV	0.2	0.1	-	0.3	0.0	0.0	0.0	0.0	0.0	0.0	0.0	0.0	0.0	0.3
Showmans goods														
5 HGV	1.0	0.1	0.1	1.2	-	-	0.1	0.1	-	-	-	-	0.1	1.3
6 Trailer HGV	-	-	-	-	0.0	0.0	-	-	0.0	0.0	0.0	0.0	-	-
Restricted														
7 HGV	3.0	0.1	-	3.2	0.0	0.0	0.1	0.1	0.0	0.0	-	-	0.2	3.4
8 HGV Farmers	0.1	-	-	0.1	0.0	0.0	-	-	0.0	0.0	0.0	0.0	-	0.1
9 HGV showmans	0.4	0.1	0.2	0.7	0.0	0.0	0.3	0.3	0.0	0.0	0.1	0.1	0.4	1.1
Others														
26 Goods (electric)[1]	0.8	0.0	-	0.8	0.0	0.0	-	-	0.0	0.0	0.0	0.0	-	0.8
60 Crown vehicles[1]	1.6	-	0.1	1.6	0.0	-	-	-	0.0	0.0	-	-	-	1.7
65-90 Exempt[1]	6.0	0.3	0.1	6.4	-	-	0.1	0.1	0.0	-	-	-	0.1	6.5
Total	264.9	27.5	20.0	312.4	4.0	39.4	27.7	71.0	0.4	16.0	15.9	32.3	103.3	415.7

1 Only vehicles in these taxation groups greater than 3500kg gross vehicle weight, and with goods vehicle body type.

Table 21 Goods vehicle stock: by gross vehicle weight and type of body: 1994

Thousands

Body type	Over 3.5t / Not over 7.5t	7.5t / 12t	12t / 16t	16t / 20t	20t / 24t	24t / 28t	28t / 32t	32t / 33t	33t / 37t	37t / 38t	38t	All weights
Rigid vehicles												
Panel Van	6.2	0.1	0.1	0.2	-	0.1	0.1		0.3		-	7.1
Box Van	55.7	6.5	7.8	22.6	0.6	1.1	0.1		-		-	94.5
Luton Van	2.8	0.3	0.5	0.3	-	-	-		-		0.0	4.0
Insulated Van	5.4	1.0	0.8	3.3	0.1	0.4	-		0.0		-	11.1
Van	3.8	0.3	0.6	0.5	-	-	-		-		-	5.3
Livestock Carrier	1.7	0.2	0.2	0.4	-	0.1	-		0.0		-	2.7
Float	3.1	-	-	0.1	-	-	-		-		0.1	3.4
Flat Lorry	10.9	1.8	2.2	8.8	0.6	2.1	1.2		-		-	27.6
Dropside Lorry	12.5	1.1	1.8	4.9	0.1	0.5	0.1		-		-	20.9
Tipper	22.7	1.3	3.3	8.3	0.2	8.1	12.9		-		-	56.7
Tanker	0.3	0.1	0.3	3.6	0.1	2.4	1.0		-		-	7.8
Concrete Mixer	0.1	-	0.2	0.2	-	2.8	0.1		0.0		0.0	3.4
Refuse Disposal	0.4	0.2	0.1	3.9	0.9	2.4	1.0		0.0		-	8.9
Goods	5.8	0.7	1.1	4.2	0.2	1.0	0.8		-		-	13.8
Skip Loader	0.9	0.1	0.2	4.7	0.1	0.5	0.5		0.0		0.0	6.9
Others or not known	17.9	2.3	3.5	9.8	0.5	2.3	2.0		0.0		-	38.3
All body types	150.2	15.9	22.7	75.7	3.4	24.0	19.9		0.4		0.2	312.4
Articulated vehicles[1]												
Panel Van		-		-	0.0	-	-	-	0.0	-	0.0	0.1
Box Van		0.1		0.2	0.2	1.8	0.4	2.8	0.3	5.9	-	11.9
Luton Van		-		-	-	-	0.0	-	-	-	0.0	-
Insulated Van		-		-	-	0.1	-	0.4	-	1.2	-	1.8
Van		-		-	-	0.1	-	0.1	-	0.2	0.0	0.4
Livestock Carrier		-		0.0	-	-	-	-	-	0.1	0.0	0.1
Float		-		0.0	-	-	0.0	-	0.0	-	0.0	-
Flat Lorry		-		0.2	0.1	0.6	0.1	1.4	0.1	6.9	-	9.4
Dropside Lorry		-		-	-	-	0.0	-	-	0.2	0.0	0.3
Tipper		0.1		-	-	0.1	-	0.1	-	2.3	0.0	2.6
Tanker		-		-	-	0.2	-	0.8	-	4.0	-	5.0
Concrete Mixer		0.0		-	0.0	0.0	0.0	0.0	0.0	-	0.0	-
Refuse Disposal		0.0		-	0.0	0.0	0.0	0.0	0.0	-	0.0	-
Goods		-		0.4	0.2	2.0	0.2	3.4	0.2	15.3	-	21.9
Skip Loader		-		-	0.0	-	0.0	0.0	0.0	-	0.0	-
Others or not known		0.1		0.7	0.6	4.7	0.9	8.0	0.6	34.2	0.1	49.9
Total		0.3		1.5	1.2	9.6	1.7	17.0	1.3	70.4	0.2	103.3
Rigid and articulated vehicles												
Panel Van	6.2	0.1	0.1	0.2	-	0.2	0.1	0.1	0.2	-	-	7.1
Box Van	55.8	6.5	7.9	22.9	0.9	3.0	0.5	2.8	0.3	5.9	-	106.4
Luton Van	2.8	0.3	0.5	0.3	-	-	-	-	-	-	0.0	4.0
Insulated Van	5.4	1.0	0.8	3.4	0.1	0.4	-	0.4	-	1.2	-	12.8
Van	3.8	0.3	0.6	0.5	-	0.1	-	0.1	-	0.2	-	5.7
Livestock Carrier	1.7	0.2	0.2	0.4	-	0.1	-	-	-	0.1	-	2.8
Float	3.1	-	-	0.1	-	-	-	-	-	-	0.1	3.4
Flat Lorry	10.9	1.8	2.2	8.9	0.7	2.7	1.2	1.5	0.1	6.9	-	37.0
Dropside Lorry	12.5	1.1	1.8	4.9	0.1	0.5	0.1	-	-	0.2	-	21.1
Tipper	22.7	1.3	3.3	8.3	0.2	8.1	13.0	0.1	-	2.3	-	59.3
Tanker	0.3	0.1	0.3	3.6	0.1	2.6	1.1	0.8	-	4.0	-	12.8
Concrete Mixer	0.1	-	0.2	0.2	-	2.8	0.1	0.0	0.0	-	0.0	3.4
Goods	5.8	0.7	1.1	4.5	0.4	3.0	1.0	3.4	0.2	15.3	-	35.7
Skip Loader	0.9	0.1	0.2	4.7	0.1	0.5	0.5	0.0	0.0	-	0.0	7.0
Special Mobile Unit	0.1	-	-	0.1	-	-	-	0.0	0.0	-	0.0	0.3
Others or not known	18.0	2.3	3.5	10.5	1.1	7.1	2.8	8.0	0.6	34.2	0.2	88.2
All body types	150.4	16.0	22.8	77.2	4.6	33.5	21.6	17.2	1.6	70.4	0.4	415.7

1 Body type refers to that of the trailer, or most frequently used trailer.

Table 22 Goods vehicle stock: by GVW [1] and year of 1st registration: 1994

Thousands

Year of first registration	Over / Not over	3.5t / 7.5t	7.5t / 12t	12t / 16t	16t / 20t	20t / 24t	24t / 28t	28t / 32t	32t / 33t	33t / 37t	37t / 38t	38t	All weights
Rigid vehicles													
1984 and before		25.8	3.0	4.9	10.3	0.4	4.0	2.6		0.1		0.1	51.2
1985		9.6	1.0	1.4	5.0	0.1	1.6	1.1		-		-	19.8
1986		10.5	1.3	1.8	5.7	0.2	1.8	1.4		-		-	22.8
1987		13.0	1.4	2.2	7.2	0.3	2.2	1.9		-		-	28.3
1988		16.6	1.4	2.5	9.4	0.4	2.8	2.8		-		-	36.0
1989		17.9	1.8	2.5	9.8	0.5	3.4	3.3		0.1		0.0	39.3
1990		14.4	1.6	2.1	7.5	0.4	2.2	1.5		-		0.0	29.7
1991		10.1	1.0	1.4	4.6	0.3	1.3	0.8		-		0.0	19.6
1992		10.0	1.1	1.3	4.6	0.3	1.1	0.8		0.1		0.0	19.2
1993		10.2	1.3	1.3	5.4	0.2	1.4	1.2		-		0.0	21.1
1994		12.2	1.0	1.3	6.2	0.4	2.1	2.4		-		0.0	25.5
All years		150.2	15.9	22.7	75.7	3.4	24.0	19.9		0.4		0.2	312.4
Articulated vehicles													
1984 and before			0.1		0.2	0.1	0.8	0.1	1.9	0.1	4.7	-	8.2
1985			-		0.1	0.1	0.5	0.1	0.9	-	3.3	-	5.0
1986			-		0.1	0.1	0.7	0.1	1.1	-	4.0	0.0	6.1
1987			-		0.1	0.1	0.9	0.1	1.4	0.1	5.9	-	8.6
1988			-		0.2	0.1	1.0	0.1	2.1	0.1	8.7	-	12.4
1989			0.1		0.3	0.1	1.1	0.1	2.1	0.2	9.8	-	13.9
1990			-		0.1	0.1	0.9	0.1	1.5	0.1	6.3	-	9.2
1991			-		0.1	0.1	0.8	0.1	1.2	0.2	4.4	-	6.9
1992			-		0.1	0.1	0.9	0.1	1.3	0.1	5.5	-	8.1
1993			-		0.1	0.1	1.0	0.2	1.6	0.2	7.7	-	10.8
1994			-		-	0.1	1.0	0.5	1.9	0.2	10.1	0.1	14.0
All			0.3		1.5	1.2	9.6	1.7	17.0	1.3	70.4	0.2	103.3
Rigid and articulated vehicles													
1984 and before		25.8	3.0	4.9	10.5	0.5	4.8	2.7	2.0	0.1	4.7	0.1	59.3
1985		9.6	1.0	1.4	5.1	0.2	2.1	1.1	0.9	0.1	3.3	-	24.9
1986		10.5	1.3	1.8	5.8	0.3	2.5	1.5	1.1	0.1	4.0	-	28.8
1987		13.0	1.4	2.2	7.3	0.4	3.1	2.0	1.5	0.1	5.9	-	36.9
1988		16.6	1.4	2.5	9.6	0.5	3.9	3.0	2.1	0.1	8.7	-	48.4
1989		17.9	1.8	2.5	10.1	0.6	4.6	3.4	2.2	0.3	9.8	-	53.2
1990		14.4	1.6	2.1	7.6	0.5	3.1	1.7	1.5	0.1	6.3	-	38.9
1991		10.1	1.0	1.4	4.8	0.3	2.1	1.0	1.2	0.2	4.4	-	26.5
1992		10.0	1.1	1.3	4.7	0.4	2.0	0.9	1.3	0.2	5.5	-	27.4
1993		10.2	1.3	1.3	5.5	0.4	2.3	1.4	1.6	0.2	7.7	-	31.9
1994		12.2	1.0	1.3	6.2	0.5	3.1	2.9	1.9	0.2	10.1	0.1	39.5
All		150.4	16.0	22.8	77.2	4.6	33.5	21.6	17.2	1.6	70.4	0.4	415.7

1 GVW: Gross vehicle weight.

Table 23 Goods vehicle stock: by year of 1st registration and type of body: 1994

Thousands

Body type	1984 & before	1985	1986	1987	1988	1989	1990	1991	1992	1993	1994	All years
Rigid vehicles												
Panel Van	0.5	0.3	0.4	0.7	0.8	1.0	0.9	0.7	0.5	0.5	0.7	7.1
Box Van	8.3	4.6	5.3	7.7	11.2	12.4	9.9	7.4	8.1	9.3	10.3	94.5
Luton Van	1.3	0.3	0.3	0.4	0.4	0.4	0.3	0.2	0.1	0.1	0.1	4.0
Insulated Van	0.8	0.5	0.6	0.8	0.9	1.1	1.4	1.2	1.3	1.1	1.2	11.1
Van	1.9	0.4	0.4	0.7	0.5	0.4	0.4	0.2	0.2	0.2	0.1	5.3
Livestock Carrier	1.2	0.3	0.2	0.2	0.2	0.2	0.2	0.1	0.1	0.1	0.1	2.7
Float	2.4	0.2	0.1	0.2	0.2	0.1	0.1	-	-	-	-	3.4
Flat Lorry	8.3	2.6	2.5	2.6	3.0	3.0	1.9	0.9	0.8	0.8	1.1	27.6
Dropside Lorry	4.2	1.5	1.6	1.9	2.5	2.7	1.9	1.0	1.0	1.2	1.5	20.9
Tipper	10.5	3.8	4.4	4.9	6.9	7.9	4.8	2.9	2.3	3.1	5.1	56.7
Tanker	1.4	0.6	0.8	0.8	0.9	0.8	0.6	0.6	0.4	0.3	0.4	7.8
Concrete Mixer	0.3	0.2	0.3	0.4	0.7	0.6	0.4	0.1	0.1	0.1	0.2	3.4
Refuse Disposal	0.6	0.4	0.7	0.9	1.1	1.1	1.0	0.7	0.7	0.8	0.9	8.9
Goods	2.4	1.4	1.6	1.4	1.7	2.0	1.4	0.7	0.8	0.3	0.1	13.8
Skip Loader	1.2	0.5	0.5	0.7	0.9	1.0	0.7	0.3	0.2	0.3	0.5	6.9
Total	51.2	19.8	22.8	28.3	36.0	39.3	29.7	19.6	19.2	21.1	25.5	312.4
Articulated vehicles[1]												
Panel Van	-	-	-	-	-	-	-	-	-	-	-	0.1
Luton Van	-	-	-	-	0.0	-	-	-	-	0.0	0.0	-
Insulated Van	0.1	-	0.1	0.1	0.1	0.1	0.2	0.2	0.2	0.2	0.3	1.8
Van	0.1	-	-	0.1	-	-	-	-	-	-	-	0.4
Livestock Carrier	-	-	-	-	-	-	-	-	-	-	-	0.1
Float	-	-	-	-	-	0.0	-	-	-	0.0	0.0	-
Flat Lorry	2.2	0.9	0.8	1.0	1.2	1.0	0.7	0.4	0.4	0.4	0.5	9.4
Dropside Lorry	-	-	-	-	-	-	-	-	-	-	-	0.3
Tipper	0.3	0.2	0.2	0.2	0.4	0.3	0.3	0.1	0.1	0.2	0.3	2.6
Tanker	0.5	0.2	0.4	0.5	0.6	0.8	0.4	0.3	0.6	0.4	0.5	5.0
Concrete Mixer	0.0	0.0	0.0	0.0	-	0.0	0.0	0.0	0.0	0.0	0.0	-
Refuse Disposal	0.0	-	0.0	-	-	-	-	0.0	-	-	-	-
Goods	2.1	1.6	1.6	2.3	3.7	4.2	2.4	1.5	1.6	0.5	0.3	21.9
Skip Loader	-	-	-	-	-	-	-	-	0.0	-	-	-
Others or not known	2.5	1.6	2.5	3.8	5.0	5.7	4.2	3.3	4.0	7.3	10.0	49.9
Total	8.2	5.0	6.1	8.6	12.4	13.9	9.2	6.9	8.1	10.8	14.0	103.3
Rigid and articulated vehicles												
Panel Van	0.5	0.3	0.4	0.7	0.8	1.0	0.9	0.7	0.5	0.5	0.7	7.1
Box Van	8.7	5.0	5.7	8.4	12.6	14.0	10.9	8.4	9.3	10.9	12.5	106.4
Luton Van	1.3	0.3	0.3	0.4	0.4	0.4	0.3	0.2	0.1	0.1	0.1	4.0
Insulated Van	0.9	0.5	0.7	1.0	1.0	1.3	1.6	1.4	1.5	1.4	1.5	12.8
Van	1.9	0.4	0.4	0.7	0.6	0.4	0.4	0.2	0.2	0.2	0.1	5.7
Livestock Carrier	1.2	0.3	0.2	0.2	0.2	0.2	0.2	0.1	0.1	0.1	0.1	2.8
Float	2.4	0.2	0.1	0.2	0.2	0.1	0.1	-	-	-	-	3.4
Flat Lorry	10.5	3.5	3.3	3.6	4.2	4.0	2.6	1.3	1.2	1.2	1.5	37.0
Dropside Lorry	4.2	1.5	1.6	1.9	2.5	2.8	1.9	1.0	1.0	1.2	1.5	21.1
Tipper	10.8	3.9	4.6	5.2	7.3	8.2	5.0	3.1	2.4	3.3	5.4	59.3
Tanker	1.9	0.8	1.1	1.3	1.5	1.6	1.1	0.9	1.0	0.8	0.8	12.8
Concrete Mixer	0.3	0.2	0.3	0.4	0.7	0.6	0.4	0.1	0.1	0.1	0.2	3.4
Refuse Disposal	0.6	0.4	0.7	0.9	1.1	1.1	1.0	0.7	0.7	0.8	0.9	9.0
Goods	4.5	3.0	3.2	3.7	5.5	6.2	3.9	2.2	2.4	0.8	0.3	35.7
Skip Loader	1.2	0.6	0.5	0.7	0.9	1.0	0.7	0.3	0.2	0.3	0.5	7.0
Others or not known	8.3	3.8	5.6	7.6	8.9	10.1	8.1	5.9	6.5	10.2	13.2	88.2
Total	59.3	24.9	28.8	36.9	48.4	53.2	38.9	26.5	27.4	31.9	39.5	415.7

1 Body type refers to that of the trailer, or most frequently used trailer.

Table 24 Goods vehicle stock: by county, region and axle configuration: 1994

Thousands

County/ Region/ Country	Rigid vehicles				Articulated vehicles									
					2 axle tractor				3 axle tractor					
	2 axle	3 axle	4 axle	All	2 axle trailer	3 axle trailer	any trailer	All	2 axle trailer	3 axle trailer	any trailer	All	All	All
Cleveland	1.80	0.25	0.10	2.15	0.02	0.71	0.20	0.93	0.00	0.08	0.20	0.28	1.21	3.35
Cumbria	2.20	0.36	0.20	2.76	0.04	0.95	0.20	1.20	-	0.34	0.37	0.71	1.91	4.67
Durham	2.06	0.29	0.27	2.61	0.10	0.63	0.18	0.90	-	0.15	0.23	0.39	1.29	3.90
Northumberland	0.93	0.13	0.17	1.22	0.01	0.24	0.07	0.32	0.00	0.07	0.08	0.16	0.47	1.70
Tyne and Wear	3.88	0.32	0.22	4.42	0.03	0.30	0.29	0.61	-	0.16	0.16	0.32	0.93	5.35
Northern	10.87	1.34	0.96	13.17	0.20	2.82	0.93	3.95	0.01	0.80	1.05	1.85	5.80	18.97
Humberside	2.85	0.41	0.25	3.50	0.04	1.27	0.29	1.59	-	0.73	0.62	1.36	2.95	6.45
North Yorkshire	4.95	0.72	0.38	6.05	0.05	1.14	0.33	1.51	-	0.41	0.34	0.76	2.27	8.32
South Yorkshire	6.09	0.58	0.49	7.15	0.10	0.80	0.72	1.62	0.02	0.32	0.59	0.93	2.55	9.70
West Yorkshire	13.38	0.88	0.56	14.82	0.15	1.77	1.36	3.28	0.04	0.57	0.64	1.25	4.52	19.34
Yorks and H'side	27.26	2.58	1.67	31.52	0.34	4.97	2.69	8.00	0.06	2.03	2.19	4.28	12.28	43.80
Derbyshire	4.19	0.50	0.57	5.26	0.01	0.57	0.45	1.04	-	0.23	0.29	0.51	1.55	6.81
Leicestershire	4.07	0.43	0.51	5.01	0.08	0.47	0.28	0.83	0.01	0.18	0.13	0.32	1.15	6.16
Lincolnshire	2.87	0.34	0.28	3.48	0.05	0.94	0.28	1.27	0.01	0.77	0.43	1.22	2.48	5.97
Northamptonshire	4.44	0.27	0.15	4.86	0.21	0.52	0.82	1.55	-	0.23	0.19	0.42	1.98	6.84
Nottinghamshire	5.51	0.47	0.30	6.28	0.04	0.59	0.60	1.23	-	0.21	0.29	0.50	1.73	8.00
East Midlands	21.07	2.01	1.81	24.89	0.39	3.09	2.44	5.91	0.03	1.61	1.33	2.97	8.88	33.78
Cambridgeshire	3.69	0.41	0.33	4.43	0.09	0.98	0.63	1.70	-	0.38	0.27	0.66	2.36	6.79
Norfolk	3.29	0.39	0.33	4.01	0.03	0.85	0.45	1.33	0.01	0.47	0.31	0.79	2.11	6.12
Suffolk	3.16	0.32	0.21	3.69	0.07	1.29	0.60	1.96	0.02	0.49	1.08	1.58	3.54	7.22
East Anglia	10.15	1.11	0.87	12.13	0.19	3.11	1.69	4.99	0.02	1.34	1.66	3.02	8.01	20.14
Bedfordshire	2.20	0.24	0.34	2.78	0.03	0.32	0.26	0.61	-	0.17	0.09	0.26	0.87	3.65
Berkshire	3.75	0.21	0.20	4.16	0.10	0.31	0.56	0.97	-	0.15	0.11	0.27	1.23	5.39
Buckinghamshire	3.74	0.36	0.30	4.41	0.05	0.82	0.67	1.54	-	0.18	0.20	0.39	1.92	6.33
East Sussex	2.19	0.11	0.08	2.38	0.01	0.13	0.06	0.20	-	0.07	0.03	0.10	0.30	2.68
Essex	5.85	0.65	0.73	7.23	0.05	1.09	0.68	1.82	0.02	0.59	0.45	1.06	2.88	10.11
Greater London	25.65	1.47	1.81	28.93	0.43	1.93	2.46	4.82	0.04	0.79	0.60	1.42	6.25	35.18
Hampshire	5.91	0.48	0.40	6.78	0.05	0.53	0.63	1.21	-	0.23	0.24	0.46	1.68	8.46
Hertfordshire	5.84	0.62	0.43	6.88	0.02	0.66	0.69	1.38	-	0.25	0.21	0.47	1.84	8.73
Isle of Wight	0.33	0.04	0.01	0.38	-	0.01	0.01	0.02	0.00	-	0.04	0.04	0.06	0.44
Kent	5.58	0.67	0.48	6.73	0.09	0.92	0.38	1.39	0.01	0.65	0.37	1.03	2.41	9.14
Oxfordshire	2.40	0.23	0.18	2.81	0.02	0.56	0.27	0.86	-	0.10	0.06	0.16	1.01	3.82
Surrey	4.91	0.74	0.32	5.97	0.01	0.51	0.25	0.78	0.00	0.07	0.08	0.16	0.93	6.90
West Sussex	2.08	0.15	0.18	2.40	0.02	0.11	0.15	0.29	-	0.04	0.04	0.08	0.37	2.77
South East	70.42	5.96	5.46	81.83	0.88	7.91	7.09	15.87	0.08	3.29	2.52	5.89	21.76	103.59
Avon	5.31	0.53	0.43	6.27	0.06	0.49	0.48	1.02	-	0.24	0.20	0.44	1.46	7.73
Cornwall	1.88	0.30	0.09	2.28	0.01	0.14	0.06	0.21	0.00	0.11	0.06	0.17	0.38	2.65
Devonshire	3.56	0.56	0.33	4.45	0.02	0.43	0.15	0.61	-	0.30	0.11	0.41	1.02	5.47
Dorset	2.05	0.24	0.10	2.39	0.02	0.23	0.08	0.33	-	0.11	0.03	0.15	0.47	2.86
Gloucestershire	2.03	0.38	0.19	2.59	0.03	0.34	0.12	0.49	0.01	0.17	0.10	0.27	0.76	3.35
Somerset	3.29	0.79	0.45	4.53	0.03	1.10	0.59	1.72	-	0.21	0.21	0.42	2.14	6.67
Wiltshire	4.12	0.31	0.22	4.66	0.13	0.43	0.55	1.11	-	0.14	0.18	0.32	1.43	6.09
South West	22.24	3.11	1.80	27.16	0.30	3.16	2.03	5.49	0.01	1.27	0.89	2.17	7.66	34.82

Thousands

County/ Region/ Country	Rigid vehicles				Articulated vehicles										
					2 axle tractor				3 axle tractor						
	2 axle	3 axle	4 axle	All	2 axle trailer	3 axle trailer	any trailer	All	2 axle trailer	3 axle trailer	any trailer	All	All	All	All
Hereford & Worcs	3.31	0.45	0.19	3.94	0.04	0.43	0.57	1.04	-	0.22	0.26	0.48	1.52	5.46	
Salop	2.77	0.41	0.23	3.41	0.05	0.48	0.27	0.81	-	0.26	0.29	0.55	1.36	4.77	
Staffordshire	4.78	0.52	0.45	5.74	0.15	0.81	1.04	2.00	0.01	0.42	0.38	0.81	2.81	8.55	
Warwickshire	2.39	0.19	0.13	2.72	0.11	0.29	0.52	0.92	0.01	0.19	0.16	0.37	1.29	4.01	
West Midlands	19.72	2.17	1.30	23.19	0.22	1.79	1.81	3.82	0.04	0.65	0.56	1.25	5.07	28.26	
West Midlands	32.98	3.73	2.29	39.00	0.57	3.80	4.22	8.58	0.07	1.73	1.65	3.45	12.04	51.04	
Cheshire	4.87	0.55	0.42	5.84	0.13	1.02	0.54	1.70	0.01	0.39	0.43	0.83	2.53	8.36	
Gtr Manchester	15.96	1.11	0.87	17.94	0.30	1.73	1.89	3.93	0.05	0.49	0.97	1.51	5.43	23.37	
Lancashire	8.31	0.69	0.56	9.56	0.14	1.07	0.76	1.97	0.02	0.42	0.69	1.13	3.10	12.66	
Merseyside	3.74	0.35	0.45	4.55	0.09	0.84	0.55	1.48	0.01	0.26	0.34	0.60	2.08	6.63	
North Western	32.88	2.71	2.30	37.88	0.67	4.66	3.74	9.07	0.09	1.55	2.42	4.06	13.13	51.02	
England	227.86	22.56	17.16	267.58	3.53	33.51	24.82	61.86	0.38	13.62	13.72	27.71	89.57	357.15	
Borders	0.53	0.09	0.01	0.63	0.01	0.09	0.03	0.13	0.00	0.04	0.03	0.07	0.20	0.83	
Central Scotland	1.55	0.20	0.13	1.88	0.02	0.33	0.17	0.52	-	0.11	0.16	0.27	0.79	2.67	
Dumfries & Galloway	1.08	0.14	0.09	1.30	0.04	0.23	0.04	0.31	-	0.10	0.16	0.27	0.57	1.88	
Fife	0.92	0.18	0.11	1.21	0.01	0.20	0.07	0.28	-	0.04	0.07	0.12	0.40	1.61	
Grampian	2.30	0.46	0.25	3.01	0.01	0.94	0.18	1.12	-	0.42	0.18	0.60	1.73	4.74	
Highland	0.94	0.19	0.08	1.20	-	0.16	0.03	0.19	-	0.06	0.06	0.13	0.31	1.52	
Lothian	2.67	0.30	0.18	3.15	0.02	0.38	0.23	0.62	0.00	0.11	0.10	0.21	0.83	3.98	
Orkney	0.14	0.05	0.01	0.19	-	-	0.01	0.02	0.00	-	-	0.01	0.02	0.21	
Shetland	0.17	0.04	0.01	0.22	-	-	0.01	0.02	0.00	-	0.01	0.01	0.03	0.25	
Strathclyde	8.37	1.08	0.62	10.08	0.06	1.00	0.54	1.60	0.01	0.42	0.62	1.05	2.64	12.72	
Tayside	1.67	0.32	0.08	2.07	0.01	0.32	0.14	0.47	-	0.16	0.07	0.23	0.70	2.77	
Western Isles	0.18	0.05	0.01	0.24	0.00	0.01	0.02	0.02	0.00	0.02	-	0.02	0.05	0.28	
Scotland	20.50	3.10	1.58	25.18	0.17	3.66	1.46	5.28	0.03	1.49	1.47	2.99	8.27	33.45	
Clwyd	1.58	0.25	0.25	2.08	0.04	0.24	0.21	0.50	-	0.15	0.10	0.25	0.75	2.83	
Dyfed	1.87	0.29	0.13	2.28	0.02	0.28	0.08	0.37	-	0.11	0.10	0.21	0.59	2.87	
Gwent	1.84	0.19	0.14	2.17	0.08	0.42	0.21	0.71	0.01	0.13	0.09	0.23	0.93	3.11	
Gwynedd	1.09	0.12	0.10	1.31	0.01	0.04	0.03	0.08	-	0.02	0.04	0.06	0.14	1.45	
Mid Glamorgan	1.67	0.25	0.18	2.09	0.05	0.30	0.17	0.52	-	0.05	0.04	0.09	0.61	2.70	
Powys	1.03	0.19	0.06	1.27	0.01	0.10	0.05	0.16	0.00	0.05	0.03	0.08	0.24	1.51	
South Glamorgan	1.61	0.11	0.05	1.78	0.01	0.18	0.06	0.25	0.00	0.06	0.04	0.10	0.35	2.13	
West Glamorgan	1.05	0.10	0.06	1.21	0.01	0.11	0.07	0.18	-	0.05	0.06	0.11	0.29	1.50	
Wales	11.75	1.49	0.97	14.20	0.23	1.67	0.87	2.76	0.02	0.62	0.49	1.13	3.89	18.09	
County unknown	0.35	0.05	0.01	0.41	-	0.08	0.02	0.10	0.00	0.03	0.03	0.06	0.16	0.56	
No current keeper vehicle under disposal	4.49	0.28	0.25	5.02	0.06	0.44	0.49	0.99	-	0.23	0.18	0.41	1.40	6.42	
Great Britain	264.94	27.47	19.98	312.39	3.99	39.36	27.66	71.00	0.42	15.99	15.88	32.29	103.29	415.67	

Table 25 Goods vehicle stock at end of year: 1984-1994: by year of 1st registration

Thousands

Rigid vehicles

Year of 1st registration	1984	1985	1986	1987	1988	1989	1990	1991	1992	1993	1994
Pre 1976	55.5										
1976	19.2	55.1	54.0								
1977	25.0	19.9		61.6	71.4						
1978	34.9	29.5	23.6			73.8	62.9				
1979	45.6	41.0	35.4	30.3				57.6	57.9		
1980	38.3	35.8	32.3	28.7	24.1					63.7	51.2
1981	29.0	28.0	26.2	24.2	21.4	18.4					
1982	29.3	28.7	27.7	26.3	24.4	21.7	17.5				
1983	33.3	32.8	32.1	31.3	29.7	27.4	23.4	19.4			
1984	36.4	35.1	34.6	34.1	33.1	30.9	27.4	23.5	20.5		
1985		35.6	36.4	36.1	35.2	33.9	31.2	28.1	25.1	22.4	19.8
1986			38.8	36.4	35.8	34.7	33.2	30.5	28.0	25.4	22.8
1987				37.6	37.8	37.3	35.9	34.2	32.2	30.4	28.3
1988					44.0	44.5	43.1	41.5	39.8	38.1	36.0
1989						45.1	44.8	43.4	42.2	41.2	39.3
1990							33.8	31.6	31.2	30.8	29.7
1991								20.0	20.2	20.2	19.6
1992									19.1	19.7	19.2
1993										20.6	21.1
1994											25.5
All years	346.5	341.3	341.1	346.5	357.0	367.6	353.3	329.9	316.2	312.5	312.4

Articulated vehicles

Year of 1st registration	1984	1985	1986	1987	1988	1989	1990	1991	1992	1993	1994
Pre 1976	4.7										
1976	3.5	5.0	5.9								
1977	6.3	4.3		8.7	11.5						
1978	10.3	7.9	5.8			11.5	9.4				
1979	13.9	11.6	9.3	7.7				8.9	9.5		
1980	10.4	9.1	7.8	6.6	5.2					10.8	8.2
1981	8.4	7.8	7.0	6.2	5.2	3.9					
1982	9.7	9.4	9.0	8.3	7.4	6.1	4.4				
1983	10.9	10.6	10.3	9.9	9.1	7.8	6.0	4.4			
1984	12.5	11.9	11.7	11.5	11.0	10.1	8.4	6.7	0.0		
1985		12.8	12.8	12.7	12.3	11.7	10.5	8.7	0.0	6.0	5.0
1986			13.7	12.6	12.4	11.8	11.0	9.7	0.0	7.1	6.1
1987				13.9	14.0	13.6	12.8	11.9	0.0	9.7	8.6
1988					16.7	16.7	16.2	15.4	0.0	13.3	12.4
1989						17.2	16.8	16.3	0.0	14.7	13.9
1990							11.1	10.2	0.0	9.5	9.2
1991								7.4	0.0	7.2	6.9
1992									8.5	8.4	8.1
1993										10.7	10.8
1994											14.0
All years	90.7	90.4	93.5	97.9	104.6	110.4	106.5	99.7	98.7	97.5	103.3

Rigid and articulated vehicles

Year of 1st registration	1984	1985	1986	1987	1988	1989	1990	1991	1992	1993	1994
Pre 1976	60.2										
1976	22.7	60.1	59.9								
1977	31.3	24.2		70.3	82.9						
1978	45.2	37.4	29.3			88.1	72.3				
1979	59.5	52.6	44.8	37.9				66.4	67.4		
1980	48.7	44.9	40.1	35.2	29.3					74.5	59.3
1981	37.4	35.8	33.2	30.4	26.6	22.3					
1982	39.0	38.0	36.7	34.6	31.8	27.7	21.9				
1983	44.1	43.4	42.4	41.2	38.8	35.2	29.4	23.9			
1984	48.9	47.0	46.4	45.5	44.0	41.0	35.8	30.3	0.0		
1985		48.4	49.2	48.7	47.5	45.5	41.7	36.8	0.0	28.5	24.9
1986			52.5	48.9	48.2	46.5	44.2	40.2	0.0	32.6	28.8
1987				51.4	51.7	50.9	48.7	46.1	0.0	40.2	36.9
1988					60.7	61.2	59.3	56.9	0.0	51.4	48.4
1989						62.3	61.6	59.8	0.0	55.9	53.2
1990							44.8	41.8	0.0	40.3	38.9
1991								27.4	0.0	27.4	26.5
1992									0.0	28.0	27.4
1993										31.3	31.9
1994											39.5
All years	437.1	431.7	434.6	444.4	461.6	478.0	459.7	429.6	414.9	410.1	415.7

Table 26 Goods vehicle stock at end of year: 1984-1994: by gross vehicle weight

Thousands

Over	Not over	1984	1985	1986	1987	1988	1989	1990	1991	1992	1993	1994
Rigid vehicles												
3.5t	7.5t	145.7	146.9	150.8	155.0	161.9	169.5	166.2	157.8	152.0	151.4	150.2
7.5t	12t	32.7	29.3	26.4	24.9	23.3	22.0	20.1	18.5	17.2	16.6	15.9
12t	16t	46.6	42.8	39.2	36.7	34.5	32.2	29.2	26.0	24.3	23.5	22.7
16t	20t	77.4	78.5	80.1	82.8	86.7	89.9	87.1	80.9	77.9	75.6	75.7
20t	24t	1.1	0.9	1.0	1.4	1.8	2.1	2.4	2.5	2.7	3.0	3.4
24t	28t	26.1	25.6	25.6	26.2	27.2	28.3	26.6	24.5	23.3	23.2	24.0
28t	32t	16.8	17.2	17.9	19.4	21.6	23.5	21.5	19.5	18.6	18.5	19.9
32t		0.1	0.1	0.1	0.1	0.1	0.2	0.2	0.2	0.2	0.6	0.6
All weights		346.5	341.3	341.1	346.5	357.0	367.6	353.3	329.9	316.2	312.5	312.4
Articulated vehicles												
3.5t	16t	0.6	0.6	0.6	0.5	0.5	0.5	0.5	0.4	0.3	0.3	0.3
16t	20t	4.9	4.5	4.1	3.7	3.1	2.8	2.4	2.1	1.9	1.7	1.5
20t	24t	0.9	1.0	1.1	1.1	1.1	1.0	1.1	1.0	1.1	1.1	1.2
24t	28t	5.4	6.3	7.3	8.4	9.1	9.7	9.7	9.2	9.3	9.3	9.6
28t	32t	2.5	1.8	1.5	1.3	1.1	1.1	0.9	0.9	1.0	1.1	1.7
32t	33t	55.7	48.7	43.7	40.5	37.3	33.5	28.1	23.2	19.9	18.1	17.0
33t	37t	1.2	1.2	1.3	1.3	1.2	1.5	1.4	1.5	1.7	1.5	1.3
37t	38t	19.4	26.3	33.9	41.2	51.1	60.3	62.5	61.3	63.5	64.4	70.4
38t		-	-	-	-	-	-	-	-	-	-	0.2
All weights		90.7	90.4	93.5	97.9	104.6	110.4	106.5	99.7	98.7	97.5	103.3
Rigid and articulated vehicles												
3.5t	7.5t	146.0	147.2	151.0	155.3	162.1	169.8	166.4	158.1	152.2	151.6	150.4
7.5t	12t	33.0	29.5	26.6	25.1	23.4	22.1	20.2	18.5	17.2	16.6	16.0
12t	16t	46.7	42.9	39.3	36.8	34.6	32.4	29.3	26.1	24.4	23.6	22.8
16t	20t	82.3	82.9	84.2	86.4	89.8	92.6	89.5	83.0	79.8	77.2	77.2
20t	24t	2.0	2.0	2.1	2.5	2.8	3.1	3.4	3.5	3.8	4.1	4.6
24t	28t	31.5	31.9	32.9	34.5	36.3	38.1	36.3	33.7	32.7	32.5	33.5
28t	32t	19.2	19.0	19.4	20.7	22.7	24.6	22.4	20.4	19.5	19.6	21.6
32t	38t	76.4	76.2	79.0	83.1	89.7	95.5	92.2	86.2	85.3	84.6	89.2
38t		0.1	0.1	-	-	-	-	-	-	-	0.2	0.4
All weights		437.1	431.7	434.6	444.4	461.6	478.0	459.7	429.6	414.9	410.1	415.7

Table 27 Goods vehicles stock at end of year: 1989-1994: by gross vehicle weight, axle configuration

Thousands

Axles	Year	Over Not over	3.5 7.5	7.5 12	12 16	16 20	20 24	24 28	28 32	32 33	33 37	37 38	38	All weights
Rigid vehicles														
2 Axle	1989		169.9	21.6	33.1	87.1	-	-	-	-	-	-	-	311.7
	1990		167.5	20.2	30.1	85.1	-	-	-	-	-	-	-	302.9
	1991		160.3	18.5	26.7	79.1	0.1	0.3	0.2	-	-	-	-	285.2
	1992		155.3	17.2	25.0	76.9	0.1	0.3	0.2	-	-	-	-	275.0
	1993		151.3	16.6	23.5	75.4	0.1	0.2	0.2	0.2	0.3	-	0.2	268.0
	1994		150.1	15.9	22.6	75.3	0.1	0.2	0.1	0.2	0.2	0.0	0.2	264.9
3 Axles	1989		0.1	-	0.1	0.3	2.1	26.8	-	-	-	-	-	29.4
	1990		0.1	-	0.1	0.3	2.3	25.6	-	-	-	-	-	28.4
	1991		0.1	-	0.1	0.3	2.4	23.5	-	-	-	-	-	26.4
	1992		0.1	-	-	0.2	2.7	22.9	-	-	-	-	-	26.0
	1993		0.1	-	-	0.2	2.9	22.8	-	-	-	-	-	26.1
	1994		0.1	0.0	0.0	0.4	3.3	23.6	0.0	0.0	0.0	0.0	0.0	27.5
4 Axles	1989		-	-	-	-	-	0.3	22.3	-	-	-	-	22.6
	1990		-	-	-	-	-	0.2	20.6	-	-	-	-	20.8
	1991		-	-	-	-	-	0.2	18.6	-	-	-	-	18.8
	1992		-	-	-	-	-	0.2	18.3	-	-	-	-	18.5
	1993		-	-	-	-	-	0.1	18.3	-	-	-	-	18.5
	1994		0.0	0.0	0.0	0.0	0.0	0.2	19.7	0.0	0.0	0.0	0.0	20.0
All	1989		170.0	21.6	33.3	87.4	2.4	27.7	22.6	-	-	-	-	365.0
	1990		167.6	20.2	30.2	85.4	2.5	26.2	20.9	-	-	-	-	353.0
	1991		160.4	18.6	26.8	79.3	2.6	24.0	18.8	-	-	-	-	330.5
	1992		155.4	17.3	25.0	77.1	2.8	23.4	18.5	-	-	-	-	319.5
	1993		151.4	16.6	23.5	75.6	3.0	23.2	18.5	0.2	0.3	-	0.2	312.5
	1994		150.2	15.9	22.7	75.7	3.4	24.0	19.9	0.2	0.2	0.0	0.2	312.4
Articulated vehicles														
2 Axle	1989			0.5		2.6	0.9	9.2	0.9	30.8	1.2	34.6	-	80.8
tractive	1990			0.5		2.3	1.0	9.0	0.8	26.1	1.2	34.8	-	75.7
units	1991			0.4		2.0	1.0	8.8	0.7	21.3	1.3	33.5	-	69.0
	1992			0.3		1.8	1.0	8.8	0.9	18.4	1.5	34.8	-	67.5
	1993			0.3		1.7	1.1	9.1	1.1	17.7	1.3	35.9	-	68.3
	1994		0.2	0.0	0.1	1.5	1.2	9.4	1.7	16.6	1.1	39.2	0.0	71.0
3 Axles	1989			-		-	-	0.1	-	0.3	0.1	23.4	-	23.9
tractive	1990			-		-	-	0.1	-	0.3	0.2	25.3	-	25.8
units	1991			-		-	-	0.1	-	0.3	0.2	25.1	-	25.7
	1992			-		-	-	0.2	-	0.3	0.2	26.7	-	27.3
	1993			-		-	-	0.2	-	0.4	0.2	28.5	-	29.3
	1994		0.0	0.0	0.0	0.0	0.0	0.1	0.0	0.4	0.2	31.2	0.2	32.3
All	1989			0.5		2.6	0.9	9.3	0.9	31.0	1.4	57.9	-	104.7
	1990			0.5		2.3	1.0	9.1	0.8	26.4	1.3	60.1	-	101.5
	1991			0.4		2.0	1.0	8.9	0.7	21.6	1.5	58.6	-	94.7
	1992			0.3		1.9	1.0	8.9	0.9	18.6	1.6	61.5	-	94.8
	1993			0.3		1.7	1.1	9.3	1.1	18.1	1.5	64.4	-	97.5
	1994		0.2	0.0	0.1	1.5	1.2	9.6	1.7	17.0	1.3	70.4	0.2	103.3

Notes and Definitions

1. NOTES ON THE VEHICLE INFORMATION DATABASE

1.1 The Vehicle Information database (VID), is held in the Department of Transport's Statistics Directorate and updated quarterly using information supplied by DVLA. The results in this publication were produced from the VID and conform to the same standards and definitions as the earlier vehicle censuses. For technical reasons the results are considered slightly more reliable than earlier estimates.

1.2 Some vehicles have complicated licensing histories, that may include incidents such as cheques failing to clear, changes of taxation status, late payments, and one or more valid or invalid refund claims. The VID undertakes a more detailed examination of licensing history and is therefore able to provide better estimates of licensed stock on a particular date than were available from the earlier vehicle census analyses.

2. NOTES ON CURRENTLY LICENSED STOCK STATISTICS: TABLES 1 to 8

Effects of using the Vehicle Information Database

2.1 The net effect of the change to the VID as the main source of statistics on currently licensed stock was to produce a small reduction - of the order of 1% - in the estimated levels of licensed stock. Although this is a small change in absolute terms, it is relatively large compared to the annual growth in licensed stock, which, since 1983, has averaged roughly 2.3% per annum.

2.2 A number of main tables showing time series of licensed stock have therefore been broken at 1992, and show both the series based on previous census analyses up to 1992, and 1992, 1993 and 1994 results taken from the VID. Estimates of changes between years before and after 1992 can be made by combining the changes from the two series.

Census methods used in earlier publications

2.3 Censuses based entirely on the record of licensed vehicles at DVLA began on 31 December 1978, and subsequent counts have been taken on the last day of the year up to and including 31st December 1992. There are two important differences between the censuses based entirely on DVLA records and censuses prior to 1978.

2.4 Firstly, censuses derived from DVLA records were based on a single point (one day) in time. In previous censuses, for purely administrative reasons, counts of licensed vehicles at Local Taxation Offices included any vehicle licensed for at least one month during the third quarter of the year.

2.5 Secondly, the DVLA-based censuses relied on a complete count of all vehicles, subject only to the complexities of establishing accurately the licensing status of the vehicle, whereas before 1978, information on vehicle stock had been obtained mainly from a sample.

Taxation class changes

2.6 There have been two major changes in recent years. Firstly, as from 1 October 1982, all general goods vehicles less than 1,525 kgs unladen weight were assessed for vehicle excise duty at the same rate as private vehicles, and the old `private car and van' taxation class was replaced by the new `Private and Light Goods' (PLG) taxation class. In addition, goods vehicles greater than 1,525 kgs unladen weight were to be taxed with reference to their gross vehicle weight and axle configuration, as opposed to unladen weight as in previous years. Farmers' light goods vehicles and showmen's light goods vehicles, i.e. vehicles of less than 1,525 kgs unladen weight, were allocated to their own distinct taxation classes and were not included in the PLG taxation class.

2.7 Secondly, as from 1 October 1990, goods vehicles less than 3,500 kgs gross vehicle weight were transferred from the `Goods Vehicle' taxation class to  the `Private and Light Goods' class. Farmers' and showmen's goods vehicles of less than 3,500 kgs gross vehicle weight, but more than 1,525 kgs unladen weight, were transferred to the `Light Goods Farmers' and `Light Goods Showmen's' taxation classes. Further proposals to reform and simplify the vehicle taxation system were announced in the November 1994 budget. The changes will take effect from 1st July 1995 and do not effect the results published in this report.

Correction for taxation class changes

2.8 The changes described above created discontinuities in the time series for vehicles currently licensed. To correct for these discontinuities, retrospective estimates of `Private and Light Goods' and `Goods' have been made for the years before 1991 using the assumption that all general goods vehicles of less than 3,500kgs gross vehicle weight would have been taxed as `Private and Light Goods'. Private cars taxed within `Private and Light Goods' have been estimated pro-rata on the basis of information on the proportion of cars within `Private and Light Goods' available for the first time in 1983.

2.9 Between 1978 and 1982, the distribution of private cars, within `Private and Light Goods', by engine capacity has been estimated pro-rata by allocating retrospective estimates for total private cars within `Private and Light Goods' across previous distributions of `private cars and vans' by engine capacity.

2.10 As mentioned above, since October 1982 gross vehicle weight has been the basis of taxation for goods vehicles. Analyses of the stock of goods vehicles by gross weight have been compiled since the 1983 census. Pre-1983 time series analysed by gross vehicle weight are not available.

Regional analysis

2.11 The only regional information easily obtainable from vehicle records held on computer by DVLA is the post code of the registered keeper of the vehicle. This can be used to determine the county in which the keeper lives. The county and regional analyses throughout this report have been compiled in this way. Vehicles under disposal are those where the previous owner has sold the vehicle and notified DVLA, but the new keeper has not completed and returned his part of the registration document. For such vehicles the post code of the registered keeper is unknown.

3. NOTES ON VEHICLES REGISTERED FOR THE 1ST TIME: TABLES 10 to 13

Sources

3.1 The statistics in this section are based on a complete analysis of new registrations and not on a sample count. Monthly analyses are compiled from the records of the Driver and Vehicle Licensing Agency (DVLA) by its IT contractor, and forwarded to the Department of Transport's Statistics Directorate.

Correction for taxation class changes

3.2 To correct for taxation class changes, as described under sections 3.6 and 3.7 above, retrospective estimates of `Private and Light Goods' and `General Goods' were made for 1969 to 1982 by assuming that all `general goods' vehicles less than 1,525 kgs unladen vehicle weight would have been registered as PLG prior to 1 October 1982, if that taxation class had been in operation. A second set of retrospective estimates was made for 1980 to 1990 assuming that general goods vehicles of less than 3,500 kgs gross weight would have been registered as PLG.

3.3 From 1975 onwards, estimates have been made of the number of private cars taxed within the `Private and Light Goods' class. Up to 1982 general goods vehicles and farmers' goods were taxed on their unladen weight and analyses were produced on this basis. Since 1983 gross vehicle weight has been the basis of taxation and new registrations have been analysed by gross vehicle weight.

4. NOTES ON HISTORIC SERIES: TABLES 9 AND 14

Motor vehicles currently licensed: census methods

4.1 Up to 1974, the figures for motor vehicles currently licensed were compiled from information received by the Department of Transport from all registration/licensing authorities or Local Taxation Offices (County, County Borough and Borough Councils) in Great Britain which administered the Vehicles (Excise) Act 1971.

4.2 Since October 1974, all new vehicles have been registered at the Driver and Vehicle Licensing Agency (DVLA), and records for older vehicles have also been transferred there, the process being completed in March 1978. For 1975 and 1976 the census was based on a combination of records held at Local Taxation Offices and at DVLA. Because of the closure of Local Taxation Offices it was not possible to produce census results in 1977. This system was superseded by censuses based entirely on the record of licensed vehicles at DVLA on 31 December 1978. Differences between censuses based entirely on DVLA records and those prior to 1978 are described in sections 3.4 and 3.5.

4.3 These differences meant that there was a discontinuity in the stock figures in 1978. Pre-1978 figures have therefore been adjusted to make them broadly comparable with those for subsequent years. These adjustments have been applied after the estimation described under `correction for taxation class changes'.

Correction for taxation class changes

4.4 The changes described above under 3.6 and 3.7 created a discontinuity in the time series for vehicles currently licensed. To correct for this discontinuity, retrospective estimates of `Private and Light Goods' and `Goods' have been made for the years 1950 to 1982, using the assumption that all general goods vehicles of less than 3,500kgs gross vehicle weight would have been taxed as `Private and Light Goods' if this class had existed prior to 1983. Private cars taxed within `Private and Light Goods' have been estimated pro-rata on the basis of information on the proportion of cars within `Private and Light Goods' available for the first time in 1983.

4.5 The `Goods' category retains farmers' goods vehicles and showmen's goods vehicles of less than 1,525kgs unladen weight. From 1983, retrospective counts of vehicles within the new taxation class groupings were produced. Other taxation classes were unaffected by the change in goods vehicle taxation.

Motor vehicles registered for the first time

4.6 Statistics in this table are based on a complete analysis of new registrations and not on a sample count. In the past these were obtained from monthly returns of licensing authorities' records of new registrations. On 1 October 1974 the Driver and Vehicle Licensing Centre (DVLC) at Swansea took over responsibility for the licensing of vehicles from Local Taxation Offices (LTO). Initially, DVLC dealt only with new registrations, but from 1 April 1975 they began to take on the registration of older vehicles from the Local Vehicle Licensing Offices, which replaced the LTOs. On 1 April 1990, DVLC became the Driver and Vehicle Licensing Agency (DVLA).

Correction for taxation class changes

4.7 To correct for taxation class changes, retrospective estimates of `Private and Light Goods' and `General Goods' have been made for 1951 to 1982 by assuming that all `general goods' vehicles less than 3,500kgs gross vehicle weight would have been registered as `Private and Light Goods' prior to 1 October 1982, if that taxation class had been in operation. The `Goods Vehicles' taxation class retains farmers' goods vehicles and showmen's goods vehicles less than 1,525kgs unladen weight. From 1975 onwards, estimates have been made of the number of private cars taxed within the `Private and Light Goods' class. Other taxation classes were unaffected by the change in goods vehicle taxation.

5.   NOTES ON GOODS VEHICLE STATISTICS: TABLES 18 TO 27

5.1 The purpose of tables 18 to 27 is to provide detailed information on heavy goods vehicles in terms of their GVW and axle configuration. This population of vehicles at the end of 1994 amounts to some 416,000 vehicles, compared with 434,000 vehicles in goods vehicle taxation groups.

Goods vehicles statistics in this publication

5.2 The goods vehicle statistics provided in tables 18 onwards cover those goods vehicles over 3.5 tonnes gross vehicle weight (GVW), in taxation groups 1 - 9, that is HGV, trailer HGV and restricted HGV taxation groups for general goods, showman's goods and farmer's goods and

52

taxation group 26 - goods (electric). In addition, results include vehicles in taxation group 60, crown vehicles, and groups 65 - 90, vehicles with various forms of exemption, provided they exceed 3.5 tonnes gross vehicle weight and have goods vehicle body type. Further information on taxation groups is given in table 3.

Goods vehicle statistics in earlier publications

5.3 Previous publications of `Goods Vehicles In Great Britain' were based primarily on results taken from the Goods Vehicle List (GVL), a register of vehicles over 3.5 tonnes gross weight licensed to carry goods on the public road network, and maintained by the DVLA. This list is a count of goods vehicles (greater than 3.5 tonnes gross weight) designed to provide a sampling population for the Continuing Survey of Road Goods Transport (CSRGT). However, some tables in that publication were drawn from the `Goods Vehicle Census', as described below.

5.4 Following the Armitage inquiry, the maximum weight limit for articulated vehicles was increased from 32.5 tonnes gross vehicle weight (GVW) to 38 tonnes GVW, effective from 1 May 1983. To monitor the effect of this change the Goods Vehicle Census, a new source of information on goods vehicles greater than 3.5 tonnes GVW and 1,525kgs unladen weight (ULW), was developed based on the DVLA register. It was designed to produce detailed information on heavy goods vehicles in terms of their GVW and axle configuration. This census included goods vehicles in a wider range of tax classes than the Goods Vehicle List, including certain goods vehicles in exempt classes.

5.5 Earlier editions of `Goods Vehicles In Great Britain' explained how it was possible to reconcile the alternative estimates of goods vehicle stock provided by the two sources. After allowing for the differences in coverage the two estimates are close, the differences being attributable to the timing of the counts. The Goods Vehicle Census is taken six weeks after the end of the year census day to allow for the processing lag between application for licence and entry into the register. The GVL counts are taken on the last day of each calendar quarter since timely counts are needed for the CSRGT. Because of its use in sampling active vehicles the GVL contains recently unlicensed vehicles which may be in the process of relicensing.

6. TAXATION CLASS DEFINITIONS

6.1 In general the classes of vehicle are based on the taxation classes set out in schedules to the Vehicle (Excise) Act 1971, although in some cases they have been renamed.

Agricultural tractors and machinery

6.2 Agricultural tractors and other self propelled agricultural machinery which are used for certain defined purposes connected with agriculture and forestry are all taxed at a special rate £30 per annum at the end of December 1993. This taxation class also includes machinery, works trucks, mobile cranes and mowing machines which make little use of public roads.

Crown vehicle scheme

6.3 All vehicles owned by Government Departments apart from those belonging to the Armed Forces are registered but pay no tax under the Vehicles (Excise) Act. Most of these operate under Certificates of Crown ownership.

Farmer's goods vehicles

6.4 Vehicles registered in the name of a person engaged in agriculture and used on roads solely for the conveyance of the produce of, and requisites for, his agricultural land.

General haulage and showmen's tractors

6.5 A general haulage tractor is used for general haulage on the public highway; it may not be used for transporting goods except on the trailer which it is towing. A similar definition applies to showmen's tractors but with the added proviso that they may be used only for towing showmen's equipment.

Goods vehicles

6.6 Mostly goods vehicles over 3,500kgs gross vehicle weight but this category also includes farmers' and showmen's goods vehicles (see below) that are less than 3,500kgs.

Motorcycles, scooters and mopeds

6.7 No distinction between these different types of machine is made for taxation purposes. It is not possible to distinguish between motor scooters and motorcycles, and although many vehicles in the size category not over 50cc are mopeds, this is only a rough guide. Furthermore, from 1965, machines used with a sidecar cannot be distinguished since they are now subject to the same rates of tax as for solo machines.

Exempt vehicles

6.8 There are some vehicles designed and used for particular purposes which are registered when they are first brought into use but which pay no vehicle excise duty. Amongst these, three types (fire appliances, ambulances and road rollers) do not carry a licence disc and their exemption is indefinite without renewal. Others (e.g. invalid vehicles, snow ploughs, certain road construction vehicles) have their exemption from duty renewed annually and carry a licence disc.

6.9 The exempt vehicle statistics exclude cars and motor cycles used temporarily in Great Britain before being privately exported under the personal export and direct export schemes by non-United Kingdom citizens. Electric vehicles have been exempt from taxation since April 1980, and are included in the exempt vehicle statistics.

6.10 Since 1979 the figures include two classes of exempt vehicles which were not previously included; vehicles which make no use of public roads (tax class 61) and vehicles which make limited use of public roads (tax class 62).

Private and light goods

6.11 Includes all vehicles used privately. Mostly consists of private cars (whether owned by individuals or companies) and vans. However, from 1 October 1990, goods vehicles less than 3,500kgs gross vehicle weight are now included in this category.

Public transport vehicles

6.12 All vehicles classified for taxation purposes as hackneys; these are vehicles used for public conveyance, i.e. buses, coaches, taxis and private hire cars. Most of these with a seating capacity of not more than 8 persons are taxis and private hire cars. Buses and coaches not licensed for public conveyance, and operated and used privately, are excluded and are classified for excise licensing with private and light goods.

Three wheelers

6.13 Mainly three-wheeled cars and vans not exceeding 450kgs unladen weight. Motorised tricycles are also included but motorcycle combinations are included with motor cycles.

Trade licences

6.14 These are issued to manufacturers and repairers of, and dealers in, motor vehicles but as they do not relate to particular vehicles they are not included in any of the tables relating to current licences or new registrations.

Vehicles owned by the Armed Forces

6.15 Vehicles officially belonging to the Armed Forces, except for a small number which for particular reasons, are licensed in the ordinary way, operate under a special registration and licensing system operated by them. Such vehicles are excluded from vehicle registration figures.

Vehicles which make limited use of public roads (tax class 62)

6.16 Vehicles which use the public roads solely for moving from one part of the owner's property to another, to an extent not exceeding 6 miles in any week, are exempted from vehicle excise on an annual basis. They have to be registered when first brought into use, but they do not carry licence discs. This exempt class has been included in the figures for `Other exempt vehicles' from 1979.

Vehicles which make no use of public roads (tax class 61)

6.17 Vehicles which are never used on public roads, that is on roads repairable at public expense, are not required to be registered unless the private roads on which they are used are roads to which the public have access (e.g. roads within railway termini). This exempt class has been included in the figures for `Other exempt vehicles' from 1979.

Symbols and conventions

.. = not available   - = negligible (less than half the final digit shown)
0 = nil (that is exactly zero) | = change or break in the series (cf table 2)

55

Printed in the United Kingdom for HMSO
Dd 298665, C3.5, 6/95, 3396, 17434 326459